FAITHLESS

FAITHLESS

SETH WALKER

MARDLE

First published in 2022 by Mardle Books
15 Church Road
London, SW13 9HE

www.mardlebooks.com

Text © 2021 Seth Walker

Paperback ISBN 9781914451058
eBook ISBN 9781914451096

All rights reserved. No part of this publication may be reproduced in any form or by any means — electronic, mechanical, photocopying, recording, or otherwise — or stored in any retrieval system of any nature without prior written permission from the copyright holders. Seth Walker has asserted his moral right to be identified as the author of this work in accordance with the Copyright, Designs and Patents Act of 1988.

A CIP catalogue record for this book is available from the British Library.

Every reasonable effort has been made to trace copyright-holders of material reproduced in this book, but if any have been inadvertently overlooked the publishers would be glad to hear from them.

Typeset by Danny Lyle

Printed in the UK

10 9 8 7 6 5 4 3 2 1

Cover image: Alamy

To my SMW. You loved me, even when I didn't like myself. You have saved me time after time, I love you more than I can ever show you.

Contains descriptions of suicide and violence.

This book is a work of non-fiction based
on the life and experiences of Seth Walker.

Certain details in this story, including names and
locations, have been changed to protect the identity
and privacy of (the author and) those mentioned.

Prologue

Born Again

Thinking that you are going to die, no, *believing* that you are going to die, is a cathartic experience.

No, that's poetic bullshit. The bitter-sweet cowardice of the Stanley knife, what a contradiction in terms. Suicide is painless... more bullshit. Red hot pain flashes at the point of the blade as I pierce the blood vessel one more time. This spurt decorates the windscreen with a bizarre inkblot test. The spurt abates to a gush and then a trickle. I swig more whisky, choke back the bile and push the knife towards my wrist again. Some cowardice hey? The blade touches an inch below the last cut. I hold my breath, I release my breath, I puke. The bile has entered my sinuses, my eyes gush, I cry and bemoan my sorry state. You worm, you insignificant, pathetic, weak-willed worm. I grab the blade, I do not look, just thrust. The crimson arc christens my lap, the legs of my jeans now resemble cowboy chaps. This time the bleeding stops within a minute. God. Blade to vein and push. God.

The time I latticed my chest and stomach with 200 surface slashes hurt, but this is another dimension of pain. I once opened my right calf down to the muscle and felt no more than a twinge, but this takes hurt to a new level.

I cannot manage another cut. I pull on the door handle, slippery with tacky blood. The February night air hits me like a slap in the face. My tears chill and make me gasp; it feels as if they're freezing.

I decide to march across Blacka Moor, to walk until I can go no further, then lie down and feed the foxes one last time. I jog, stumbling along the bridleway. My feet break the thin, icy crust of puddles with staccato snaps which echo in the clear, crisp air. I notice how sharp the sound of the ice cracking is, in contrast to that strange whine. A low keening is following me as I penetrate deeper into the darkness of the moor. I am frightened now. Tonight, for the first time in years, the night has a voice calling to me – moaning, mumbling, stuttering. I stop. I don't want to, I want to run, but my legs sag beneath me. The whine stops with me. God. I turn my head, the noise turns with me. I set off again and the harsh mewling stays. Shit, what is this fresh horror? I stop to listen; it stops with me. I begin to laugh as I realise that I have run from my own voice: I am the moaning, keening beast! I laugh as I sink my back onto a grassy tussock. I am lying, half in a puddle, half on the grass. The coldness of the water burns my arse and legs, the cool cotton wool of the grass comforts me as I look to the sky.

It's clear, and yes there are some stars.

This would be a good place to die.

As I look at the stars I start to pray. I am, after all, a priest. I ask the God I thought I had been serving for the whole of my life to give me some measure of comfort, of absolution. In the depth of my utter desolation I ask for him. In my loneliness I ask for his presence. I'm going to die, God. Here on the moors. I have fucked up big style. Just give me a sign, a feeling, a voice, a warmth.

"GIVE ME SOMETHING LORD."

Silence.

Nothing.

Void.

I cry.

Here I am in my Gethsemane on the night of betrayal. "I need you."

There is nothing.

"Help me!" I cry against the wind.

Nothing.

There must be something.

Where is the white light, the tunnel, the voices, the angels?

Nothing.

My tears, hot, salty, unholy tears baptise my face as I'm born again.

There is nothing here.

I am alone.

You bastard. You stupid, whining bastard, there is nothing here!

My tears give way to anger, "How can you abandon me?"

Then to laughter, laughter for the joke my life has been. The humour of believing in walking on water, of water to wine, of wine becoming blood and bread becoming flesh.

What a revelation.

It doesn't matter. It doesn't matter what he think;, God is not here, he isn't anywhere. It doesn't matter.

I laugh. I'm changed. I'm born again. I'm renewed.

I push down with my left arm: it buckles. I roll onto my left side and push with my good arm. I am crouching. Self-preservation is kicking in now. I realise that it doesn't matter. Who cares what people think? How ironic. I've changed my mind. I want to live.

Fuck the world.

My legs buckle and I kiss mud.

This time, come on, push. I heave myself upright and begin the walk towards the light.

Chapter 1

GOD MOVES IN A MYSTERIOUS WAY

It's difficult to think of a time before God. He was always there in some form or another, in the morning prayer of a visiting uncle, in the recital of grace before a meal, in the frantic search for us children as we desperately hid from the prospect of boring Sunday School. I thought of God then as a cuddle from a father, of recognition, of some form of affirmation. My own father, at that time, was a bundle of contradictions, happy and playful, stern and distant. To win a cuddle from Dad was quite a prize. It was like soothing ointment on my bruised psyche. It went some way to counteract the harsh comments he sometimes made.

It must have been tough, trying to find some peace with four children bouncing off each other. What I didn't realise until I became a parent myself was the hard work and pressure that parenthood brings. The weight of responsibility of providing for a household of six, plus added folk over the years, was a difficult one for him to carry, but he did it.

I later discovered how my dad had reinvented himself several times during his life as he faced career breaks, moving jobs and leaving the security of being a homeowner. One of his biggest risks was to train for the ministry during his 50s; he's still serving the church now, in his 80s.

When I was a young child in the late 60s, my dad was employed by a large pharmaceutical company. He was working on a project to develop and bring to the market a new anti-depressant. His firm was on the outskirts of a burgeoning new town, and we lived in a commuter development attached to a small country village. Opposite my dad's firm was a printing company which had one of the first seven-spot colour printing presses in the country. The pharmaceutical firm was going to use the latest in printing technology to market their new drug. But first some field testing was needed. In an innovative move, they gained permission to collaborate with a laboratory, in a European communist country.

In the 1960s the Iron Curtain was firmly in place, with no sign of it ever lifting. So there were strict protocols to follow, and the state would keep a watchful eye over my dad's movements.

As a man of faith, he knew that the church in this communist country was being persecuted by the government. It was an offence for people to openly worship, or to own certain religious books. In the Eastern Bloc, churches, synagogues and mosques had ceased to be places of worship and had been transformed by the state into museums of atheism. An estimated 12 to 20 million of the faithful found themselves victims of a godless regime, with forced labour a reality for many.

Dad saw an opportunity to reach out to his brothers and sisters in Christ, who were facing oppression. He managed to smuggle religious literature translated into their language and printed with the latest colour technology into his luggage. This was a great personal risk that he took, with implications for us as a family. If he'd been caught, he would have faced certain arrest and imprisonment. But he was true to his convictions and, despite the dangers, he stood up to be counted. This speaks volumes to me about his faith. He put it before his own career and potentially his own freedom. A further measure of the man is that I've never heard him speak of this to anyone else.

He has a strength of character that I can only aspire to emulate. I was to witness this once and hear about it on two other occasions.

It was the summer of 1986, just before I went back for my final year at theological college. I asked Dad if we could go caving one last time. I'd been caving with my dad since I was eight. As I grew older, the trips became more challenging in nature. Why did I keep going back underground? I'm not sure there's one answer to that. I do have a fear of heights and it seems to me that as I still climb today, I just want to make sure that I have control over that fear and make sure it doesn't have the better of me. Caving has certainly given me the opportunity to test my mettle, to make sure that I don't give in to the rising dread as I stand on top of a vertical pitch. There's also the sense of accomplishment that you gain from completing a trip.

Caving, like climbing, is as much a mental workout as it is a physical one. It is a series of problem-solving exercises. What line to take up a sheer rockface? Which way to take when faced with several identical openings? How to approach a tight crawl – on your back or front? Ensuring you are safe in all you do, that you apply the right controls to mitigate risk, is part of the satisfaction you gain. Another factor that explains why we do it is that we get to go where very few people venture and therefore see rare and unspoilt sights. Huge stalactites hang from the rock ceilings and columns of stalagmites grow up from the cave floor to meet them. Rich veins of minerals and crystals glisten in our lamplight; Blue John, fluorspar and quartz shine with iridescence. Those who venture underground certainly do so for different reasons, but they all share these rich rewards that surface dwellers are unaware of.

We settled on Gaping Gill in North Yorkshire's limestone country, a hole that could comfortably house Brinsley Cathedral. It is part of one of the most impressive cave systems in England and rests on the bleak flanks of

Ingleborough, one of the famed Yorkshire three peaks. There is an impressive 330ft waterfall, the biggest known in the country at that time, but underground. In the summer you can cheat and be winched to the bottom seated on a small platform, a test of nerve in itself, but definitely the easier option. We were going to go in a different way.

We would have to squirm down into the first vertical drop, known as a pitch. We would abseil down and climb back up the same ropes, using what is known as single rope technique. The first pitch is a 45ft deep vertical shaft, and it's a squeeze. Caving isn't for those who have a fear of confined spaces, or heights, or the dark. It's for people who like to challenge themselves, who like to push their own personal boundaries and witness things that only those who dare to push a little further will see.

There are several smaller pitches, climbs using fixed ropes and a ladder, thin-ledged traverses, with deep holes to avoid. The big test of nerve, however, is the yawning shaft known as big pitch: a sheer 100ft drop to a rock-strewn floor, somewhere beneath us in the all-consuming darkness. In those days we used sealed lead acid battery-powered miners' lamps, and the beam couldn't reach the bottom. I'd worry that the rope would not stretch all the way to the ground. I had visions of abseiling off the end of the rope and being smashed to pieces on the rocks below. Not this trip though. We had made it to the bottom and stood on the fringes of the great waterfall.

Once every few seconds a sheet of water would break from the main fall and blast the accumulated mud from under us, knocking us to our knees in the process. At the back of my mind, the fearful thought of the climb up the big pitch spoilt the enjoyment of the moment. It lived up to my anxious anticipation. By the time I got to the top, my chest and arms were burning from the effort of the ascent. I climbed onto the ledge, unclipped myself and shouted for my dad to ascend. How would he fare? He was in his 50s. It had taken its toll on me and I was a keen sportsman, running and playing football and rugby for my college.

It wasn't too long before I could hear the laboured breathing as he ascended into sight. When he was safely on the ledge, he unclipped, and we rested. We started to pull up the rope and load the kit.

"Hang on, Seth." My dad sounded as if something wasn't right. "My descending gear isn't here!"

This presented us with a problem. His very expensive descending gear was at the bottom of this 100ft, strength-sapping shaft. I would have left it and chalked it up to experience. Not my dad. With no safety rope, he rigged a replacement descender out of karabiners and, with a determined nod, abseiled down the shaft. 15 minutes later he was back on the edge, exhaustion etched on his face, with his precious descender safely in the kit bag.

I learned more about my dad in this one incident than in all my 22 years up to then. He had weighed up the situation, taken the risks into account and embarked on a physical and mental test that few would be willing to take. I would struggle to make the same choice, preferring to value my safety more, and would be willing to leave the expensive equipment as a gift of the cave for another lucky explorer to find.

That was not to be the last time he'd be tested underground. At the age of 60 he was with his caving partner, Robin, when he had a fall in the King's Dale system. This happened about as far from the cave entrance as you could explore. He landed hard, his back making contact with a large rock, damaging his ribs. He lay winded and in pain.

Robin made him comfortable and said that he'd go for Cave Rescue. My dad was having none of it. "I haven't called Mountain or Cave Rescue out in 40 years and I'm not starting now!" was his response. After several hours of dogged, grim progress, they made their way out. Robin asked where the nearest hospital was. My dad was having none of that, either. Although two long hours' drive away, he instead insisted, "Take me to the Macclesfield Royal. My son-in-law is a consultant in the accident and emergency department and my wife won't have far to come to visit."

When she did visit though, he greeted her with a characteristic "How's my dog?", his first thought being for his Border Collie companion.

Again, this strength of character saw him draw on his reserves of grit not only to get him out of a challenging cave system while injured and in pain, but also to ensure that he wasn't too much trouble for the rescue services – or his wife.

The third example happened when he was walking with his Border Collie, Jess, on the moors, having given up caving due to his advancing years. He cut his hand badly climbing a barbed wire fence. Past experience of his creative route-finding led me to correctly speculate that he was off path and trespassing. As usual he dodged the hospital. He phoned his son-in-law and was stitched up over his kitchen table in his own home. Proper old school is my dad.

But resilience doesn't come cheap. It's a quality which accumulates over time as you get up from one of life's knockout punches, dust yourself down and move forward once more. I've had to dig deep and draw from my own meagre inner resources to rebuild from scratch twice in my life and have taken some measure of comfort from my dad's example over the years. Even so, I'd like to be able to scale mountain peaks when I'm in my 80s as he did and hope to be able to demonstrate his strength of character when testing times come once again.

When I was a child, God, to me, was a strange mixture of my dad, Father Christmas and an imaginary friend.

It was this friend whom I fell asleep talking to every night, only it was always a one-way conversation. I suppose that the first problem in our relationship came when God could not or would not protect me.

I am cursed with a legacy from my mother, a trace of the narcolepsy that blighted her life, turning her into a nocturnal being who existed in a twilight zone. At the age of eight I began to suffer from a shadow of narcolepsy – hypnopompic hallucinations, commonly known as night terrors.

As I lay in my bed saying my prayers, I would become aware of a high-pitched noise, faintly perceptible at first, but growing to I'd begin to feel the bed being pushed down as if someone or something was moving up the bed towards my face. I was convinced that I was awake.

I now know that I was suffering from sleep paralysis, my body unable to move, my mind wide awake, desperately trying to make sense of normal physical sensations and failing miserably.

Back in my bedroom, I can feel, even now, the hot breath of something upon my face. My eyes are wide open, but I can't make anything out. The room has grown darker; suddenly a shaft of moonlight streams through a crack in the curtains, illuminating a horned goat's face. I struggle to form the name of Jesus as I cry out for his help, "Je... Je... a Jes... Jes... Jes... esus... JESUS! JESUS!"

I awake in a piss-soaked bed, too frightened to make the infinite journey from bed to light switch. I await the coming of dawn in a cooling, damp bed.

It is strange that even at this early age I was being conditioned to accept a God who would allow a little boy, defenceless, frightened and lonely, to lie awake night after night whispering his name as a talisman against his worst fears.

It never really seemed to work, the name of God. It never prevented the sense of evil that would violate my sleep night after night. Instead, the repetition of Jesus's name sowed the seeds of the obsessive-compulsive disorder that would stay with me for the next three years.

A floorboard creaks. A shadow squeezes under the door and displaces the gentle light of the landing. The door handle turns, slowly, agonisingly slowly. I reach for the covers and pull. They will not move. I am trapped. A thin shaft of light grows as the door opens. And it's there before me, revealed in full horror. Not the head of a demon, but the head of Tim. Tim, the man with several learning difficulties who Dad is teaching to read, has slipped upstairs to where the children sleep. His face is fixed with a peculiar smile. A smile which turns into a frown of disappointment as he recognises me. The door shuts, he's gone. I breathe out for the first time since the floorboard creaked and lie down to sleep. I don't hear my brother's door being opened as Tim prepares to spend some quality time with the 10-year-old. Thankfully, my dad, curious about the length of time Tim was taking to visit the toilet, called him back just as he was whispering his poisonous intent, before his words became despicable actions.

GOD MOVES IN A MYSTERIOUS WAY

Yes, God was there all right. In the routines, the visits, the admonishing, the Sunday lunches, the cuddles, the hymns, the books we read and the guilt we felt. He was the thread which held the seam of my life together. Jesus provided a focus for love and devotion, followed by a target for teenage rebellion – and the subject of a tearful reunion when I finally made my decision to turn my life back into his hands. That day, in a friend's front room, with cleansing tears baptising me, I began a journey that would prove to be a hell of a trip.

I still can't believe it was me who did those things, or saw those sights. I've held babies as they died, baptising their lifeless forms. I've released prayer balloons for dead toddlers. I've sat on urine-soaked sofas and wrestled with a drunk who believed that he was possessed by a demon. I've fought with a man whose wife would subsequently brand her toddler's face with a hot poker straight out of the coal fire. I've looked into the eyes of a self-confessed "stone-cold killer" as he told me that he wanted to make his family perfect, even if he had to stab them all to do it. I did all that and more. And less. I still don't know how or why. But it truly was one hell of a ride, one that ended, ultimately, on Blacka Moor in the company of a Stanley knife.

Chapter 2

ACID AND OUIJA

"Get away! Get away you fucker!" Billy screamed as he fought himself awake. The same dream tormented him every night. The little preacher's haunted face twisted as he desperately prayed through his tears, "Father, forgive them for they know not what they do."

He couldn't remember how long Church House had been their meeting place; years, months, weeks, days blurred and slurred. The acid and the glue had seen to that, but they were here now and they would have some fun. The preacher was small, maybe 5ft small. He had opened the house to them from day one. Billy couldn't believe it. It had started with a few small loans to them that were never paid back, then little by little they took it all from him and now they owned him.

That night was cold and wet, too wet to be out on the street. The hollow resounding knock of knuckle on wood told them that Church House was empty, it was theirs for the night. Billy, Dave, Huey and Brian climbed adeptly up the drainpipe and forced the flimsy bedroom window open. It was Brian who had shared out the acid. Small harmless looking dots on pieces of rice paper. It was Billy who had passed round the tin of glue. Minutes flared into kaleidoscopic hours. They laughed, cried and screamed through the evening, until a tap at the door announced the arrival of Big Jane.

The heavily built debutante with tattooed knuckles was at the door with a board and box tucked under her arm; the window was opened and she climbed in and laid her treasure on the table. The kitschy styled ouija board beckoned, calling with words of excitement and forbidden knowledge.

"Who's up for this? No fucking cowards!"

A glass was found. It spun around the board as teenage fingers rested upon it.

"Stop pushing the glass Billy, you knob," Jane spat.

"I'm not, honest," he replied, surprised.

It slid in jerky movements from letter to letter as it spelled out the same message again and again. It mocked, this clown, this piss-taker of a spirit. It mocked as they refused to do it, as the acid caused them to drift and doubt, as the glue deadened the command.

"Kill the preacher," Jane whispered.

"Kill the preacher?" Billy repeated in disbelief.

"Kill the preacher," it spelt i out again.

The preacher was taken from his room and led downstairs.

"Merciful Father!" the preacher exclaimed at the sight of the youths as they turned towards him, their faces adorned with felt-tip swastikas and inverted crosses. "How did you all get in here?" he enquired.

"Fuck off!" shouted Billy, to the amusement of his crew. "Fuck off and die you dirty old man!"

The preacher shuddered, praying, "Lord give me strength."

"You don't know the meaning of the word," sneered Billy as he tugged up the sleeve of his 'Anarchy' T-shirt, flexing his bicep to make the prison-tattooed phrase "Bollocks" stand out proudly, provocatively. "That's strength!" He threw back his head, belching out deep guttural laughter.

"Get out! This is the house of God!" the preacher asserted.

"No it's not," Billy countered, "This is the house of the devil!" The preacher flinched as the youth lunged at him. Side-stepping, he ran through the connecting door into the whitewashed chapel.

Feverishly he wedged a solid wooden pew under the flimsy handle and fell to the floor in fervent prayer.

"Our Father, who art in heaven…"

Crash. The sound of heavy boots striking the door interrupted his litany as the tears began to fall.

"Hallowed be thy name."

Crash.

"Thy kingdom come, thy will be done…"

Crash.

"…on earth as it is in heaven."

Crash.

"Give us this day our daily bread,"

Crash.

"Forgive us our trespasses, as we forgive those who trespass against us."

Boom! The door burst open, throwing the solid oak pew across the tiled floor.

"The bastard's praying," Billy mocked. "Say one for me," he snarled, grabbing the wooden cross that was screwed to the white-washed wall.

"And lead us not into temptation," the preacher called with fresh determination, the salty water baptising his face.

With a feral grunt Billy wrenched the crucifix from the wall.

"But deliver us from evil."

"Deliver this, bitch!" the youth snarled as he inverted the cross over the preacher's head.

"For thine is the kingdom," his voice rose with strength, "the power and the glory."

Billy faltered for an instant, then his pupils constricted to pin holes of blackness as his grip tightened.

"For ever and ever…"

Crack! "Amen."

Simultaneously the prayer ended as the twin arms of the crucifix snapped, showering the cleric with debris and breaking his resolve. His prayer was not answered.

Here he was, in the abomination of his own desolation. No one to call to. Just a void and an emptiness. Icy constriction clutched at his chest as Billy laughed again. The remains of the cross were dropped as the youths gathered round the mewing man. Silently, and almost as if choreographed, each took a limb and they carried their sacrificial lamb up the stairs, ascending to be cleansed. A bath was filled with water, cold water. The man was stripped and plunged. Under he went, and he was held there, bubbles and his cries for mercy breaking the surface. Then out, out and downstairs to his Calvary chair of crucifixion, of sacrifice. Tied to his cross, a rope in the place of nails.

A slap and Billy began the confession. "You're gay, aren't ya?" he barked.

"No, I'm not," came the reply.

"You're gay, aren't ya?" it came back again.

"No I'm..." SLAP. The sting of hand on face interrupted his reply.

"You're gay and you fuck men."

"No I..." Slap.

"You" Slap. "Are" Slap. "Gay" Slap.

"N..."

"You!" Slap. "Are!" Slap. "Gay!" Slap. The blows increased in force. The old man dipped his chin. Billy forced his chin up.

"You!" Slap. "Are!" Slap. "Gay!" Slap. "Say it, you old bastard! SAY IT!"

"Alright, I'm gay, I'm gay, I'm gay," he volunteered, offering the confession freely, repeatedly. "I'm gay." His voice trailed off and gave way to mumbling and then nothing.

"Queer fucker, where's your God now?" Billy was warming to the task. "Where's your God?" he insisted.

The churchman remained silent.

"I'm your God!" The statement was punctuated with an open-handed blow.

"Say it." His broken will gave way to a broken heart. There was nothing left. No resistance, no life, no joy, no hope.

"I'm your God." Slap. "I'm your God." Slap.

The litany was repeated until he couldn't bear it any more. From the depths of his despair and humiliation he cried, "You are my God!"

"What? I don't think I 'eard yer, fucker!"

"Fucker!" Huey spat. "Let's burn him!"

No one spoke, but shadows flitted across the room. A blanket appeared, some lighter fluid was thrust into Billy's hands. The cleric was hooded, the fluid was sprayed and sparks flew as Jane's lighter spluttered into life. Then the flame grew in strength as she reached towards the blanket.

* * *

I was told that my predecessor spent time convalescing after a tough time in the village. I never met him, he didn't return to Bluebell Common, but the consequences of what happened were significant, not least for Billy, whose life would be tied to the occupant of that house for some time to come.

When I was asked to consider living and working at Bluebell Common, it was described to me as one of the most desolate tracts of housing in England. Whether that was true or not, I have no way of evaluating. A social worker I worked with to help the families described in this book used to say that the employment rate in the village was 64 per cent. Again, I can't verify this. I do know that in my block of terraced houses and the block opposite, no one had a job. Let me clarify that; no one was employed, in a job with wages, paying tax, national insurance or pension contributions. Wiggy might mend your car for a few pounds, cash in hand. Malcolm might supply you with coal, that was already too hot to handle. Tracey might clean your club, for a brown envelope payment.

The pit had shut down, the very reason the village was built 80 years before. The knock-on effect on local businesses was huge, and small firms closed down. As the miners' weekly wage packets disappeared, the local shops, pubs and clubs lost trade. It was a downward slide into poverty and despair with no hope of a change. I was told that Bluebell Common had the shortest waiting list for a council house in the whole of the borough, and I could see why.

The nearby steelworks had closed down as the recession bit, closing off that avenue of employment for my fellow residents.

Despite European funding, little of any substance happened for our people. New businesses didn't seem to open and industry was in decline. Someone once said that if you live without hope, you stop to live. It seemed to me that hope had left Bluebell Common; the community was struggling to live.

In my ignorant naivety, I thought that I could bring hope to the village, a hope in Jesus that would bring new life to a people slowly going under.

I turned the key in the lock of Church House and made a new start on New Year's Day 1988.

I entered the building that was to be my home for the next four years. Oh yes, this is the home where the piss-taker spirit was called up, where kindness gave way to weakness, where Billy was said to have broken the cleric and where he'd also try to spill my blood.

Home sweet home.

Chapter 3

WELCOME TO THE LOST CITY

I took a deep breath, muttered a silent prayer and knocked at the grime-flecked door, which immediately swung open, presenting me with a wild-eyed, freckled man. His unkempt ginger hair framed a grimacing face, giving him an air of barbarian fury. His name was Clive, as I later discovered. "What do you fucking want?" he barked.

"Hello, my name is Seth, I live at Church House. I've come to talk about John East."

"Who sent you?" he queried harshly.

"No one," I replied. "I've come to try to help. I work for the church."

An awkward silence ensued. As the seconds ticked away I held his gaze, smiling. I didn't want him to believe I was weak, but I also didn't want to appear aggressive and provoke him into something both he and I would regret.

His expression changed, it softened. "You'd best come in then," he conceded.

The house was dark, smelly, filthy and untidy. In the midst of the mess, two young children, one naked, the other partially clothed, played and cried in turn.

"Look, I know John is supposed to have burgled your house, but that's no cause to threaten him. There's a lot more to this than meets the eye," I offered, as he stood over the chair where I sat, his nostrils flared and his fists clenched, as his anger began to surface once more.

"You see I think he's carrying the can for someone else, someone bigger than him and bigger than you."

"Oh aye, and who might that be?" He snarled his question.

"I'm not sure, but what I do know is that John's ready to do himself in rather than face a hiding from you. He's definitely not a fighter despite all his big talk, and he's afraid of what you might do to him. I'm here to appeal to your better nature, because if you go after him there's no telling what he'll do."

"Bea!" he called out towards the kitchen. "Bea! Get in here."

After a few seconds, a grey-haired, withdrawn woman who looked at least 15 years older than she really was, shuffled into the room.

"This feller is from the church, he says that I shouldn't give Easty a hiding," he explained. "He thinks that he might do himself in if I do. What do you think? It was your telly."

"Huh, I don't know," she grunted almost inaudibly.

Bea, I later discovered was suffering from depression. For years she had been pushed around by life; it was as if she had been sent to the corner of the room like a disobedient child and had stayed there, trapped by her fears. "I... I don't know."

"All right love," Clive replied, turning to face me again.

Seconds ticked away in silence. He was fighting an inner battle; what would he decide?

"Look, tell him I won't touch him. I'll let it pass, so tell him he is welcome here if he needs a friend."

To think that I had dreaded and put off that visit. It was only John East's insistence that he was suicidal that had made me search for what little courage I had and resolve to visit Clive. I couldn't believe how easy it'd been; he had looked so angry, hard even as I entered the house, and now it was like talking to a different person. But that was Clive all over, one minute calm and peaceful, the next possessed by anger as his eyes burned murderously from a face contorted with rage. He could swing from friend to foe and back to friend in one intimidating moment.

This first meeting was to be our last for a few months, until his cousin Barry came to live with him, bringing his wife and two children.

Eight of them lived there in a three-bedroomed, terraced council house on my patch, Bluebell Common estate. Clive's story is a tragic one, at times dramatic, but also a story of grace, forgiveness and generosity. It's told here largely as it happened, but with a few names and situations altered to avoid unnecessary embarrassment and trouble for me.

Clive was born in England to Irish parents. His mother died when he was four, leaving an emotional scar that ran deep, and which remains unhealed today. When I first met him, he struck me as being a hard man. Subsequent events proved this to be far from true but acted as a warning to never let fury, rage or bitterness find a place in your heart.

It was the beginning of summer; the football that I'd bought as an evangelistic tool was taking a severe bashing as several young men joined in a game on the school field. One of those men was Clive's cousin Barry. A man with a violent past and no real hope for the future. He had been resisting every attempt I'd made to get him to come to church.

"I used to do Karate at a church hall once," he'd said. "I'll come if someone will fight with me after."

"You come this Sunday and I'll have a fight with you if you want," I countered.

But he hadn't come and there seemed to be no way forward with him, until one day he was threatened by one of the real hard men on our estate and I saved him from a beating, using soothing words, not fists. He owed me one now and he knew it. So after the game I asked him to come to hear a converted street fighter preaching at an outreach meeting. Again he refused, so there was nothing else for it: I called in the favour and told him he was going and that he had ten minutes to get ready.

That night the preacher's testimony seemed to hit home. Later, Barry said it was just like hearing his own life being described; he knew then of his need for God, so he strode forward to give his life to Jesus.

From then on he began to read the Bible and he told his cousin that he needed God, too. It was a matter of just days before Clive bent the knee to the Lord. Life suddenly became easy for him; he moved to Windsor and lived a life of luxury… Wrong! He actually went on to face the most trying time of his life, a time that rocked him and shook the church's work at Bluebell Common to the core.

Clive had been involved with the church for a number of weeks, and his home life was beginning to change as we tried to convey the idea to him that his wife needed care and support, not anger, criticism and housework. She was a withdrawn and clearly depressed woman who needed a great deal of help; but how to offer it and what to offer was beyond me.

If anything, after an initial improvement, the house was getting even more filthy, as the effects of two families living in such a small space took hold. There were now nine people in the cramped three-bedroomed house, since Bea had given birth to a baby girl, called Jane. Sparks often flew as the cousins clashed, but these temporary quarrels were forgotten when tragedy struck.

Clive had gone to Ravenscliffe House to attend his employment training course, a mandatory requirement for those who had been receiving unemployment benefit for six months or more. Barry was at the probation office, waiting to get some hours of his Community Service Order worked off. The women were sleeping in. At around 11 in the morning, Barry's wife Jean had got up to see to her children. It was another hour before Bea surfaced, only to discover young Jane lying cold and stiff in her cot. She had an undiagnosed congenital heart disease, which could have taken her at any time.

The ambulance had just left as I arrived at the house after being informed via the local bush telegraph that something was wrong. The stories that were excitedly related to me as I strode up the road varied from "It were cot death" to "She strangled it you know, she in't right in the head."

Jean was clearly upset. "Bea should have got up earlier, I told her to. Now everyone is going to be after us," she blurted out in anger. After reassuring her as best I could, I raced to the hospital where Bea was.

Why am I only a lay minister, I thought, as I tried to talk my way past the hospital receptionist. If only I had a dog collar I would be straight through. I struggled to not let my frustration boil over into anger. As she went to find someone with greater authority to deal with me, I slipped out of the door and down the corridor and spotted Bea in a small lounge room being questioned by two uniformed policemen. She looked so sad and so pathetic, this small woman, old before her time. I just wanted to pick her up and carry her away from all this, to take her to a place where no one could trouble or bully her, where she could grieve in peace.

One of the policemen, a sergeant, was suspicious of me at first, but became more trusting when he heard about my involvement with the family. Taking me outside, he intimated that although there were no visible signs of abuse or violence, they were concerned about the circumstances of the child's death given the state of the house, and they wanted to more information. So I was left alone with Bea to try to find out the truth and to comfort her.

"They'll blame me won't they?" was all she offered. It was obvious she didn't know how the child had died; it was also obvious she was deeply afraid: afraid of the police, whose mood had just changed with the arrival of two plainclothes detectives, one of whom had earned the nickname of 'Bad News' Bentley among the locals. They pushed me out of the room and wouldn't let me back in. I protested that Bea had her rights and should be accompanied, but they refused to listen. 'Bad news' Bentley was questioning Bea and I could hear her crying. The room had double doors, the type you push to open. As I moved to one side, the other detective, who was guarding the doors, kept moving so that he was constantly in front of me.

"Push any harder young man, and that could be classed as assaulting a police officer."

I stopped. Stunned.

Through the doors was a depressed, bereaved woman. A victim all her life and alone in the midst of her grief, being accused of who knows what. I wasn't brave enough to try again. A parish evangelist with a criminal record wouldn't go down well with the Church of England.

I sat down to wait it out, inwardly seething at the injustice of it all. What a farce. Who knows what Bea would admit to to stop being harangued?

Clive, Barry, his wife Jean and Bea were all taken up to Bradley Police Station, where they were questioned until eight at night. Once again I was refused access to any of them; Barry especially was insisting that I be allowed in, but the police weren't interested.

Back home later that evening, Clive was visibly shaken, white and trembling, and he began to rage.

"Give it to God, he'll understand, Clive," I said, as he shook with emotion before falling to his knees and repeatedly crossing himself while praying out loud. He seemed to be calming down until he jumped to his feet with a roar and lashed out, punching an already holed door and violently kicking the fire. Leaping forward, Barry grabbed hold of his arms, pleading, "Don't smash the house up, it only hurts the girls, hit me, go on, get rid of it. Hit me!"

For an eternity of silence Clive stared at his cousin before collapsing into his arms in tears.

I was witnessing a world that had been hidden to me all my privileged life, and I didn't like it. Throughout our country an underclass was merely existing, bouncing along the bottom, barely surviving. They weren't statistics, they were real people, broken by the worst of what life on the lowest rung had to offer. I never knew such poverty existed in the 1980s until I entered the lost world of Bluebell Common.

Sometimes I wished I worked in an office, or maybe as a road sweeper – at least there wouldn't be all this, I thought, as I drove towards the hospital. Clive was about to view his daughter's body at the chapel of rest; it was surely going to be an emotionally charged event. Three years at theological college and a degree in Theology and Philosophy was no preparation for this.

The coroner, his assistant, a nurse, two policemen, Barry and Clive were waiting in the hospital basement. The march down to the chapel was a quiet one other than the sound of heavy police shoes echoing on the hard floor, Clive's harsh shallow breathing and the jangle of the coroner's keys. All too soon we were there. Swallowing hard, I went in. A kind of peace descended as, tenderly, Clive reached out towards his child, a peace that was short lived as he cried out, "No, No, No!"

He was again racked with loud sobs and had to be half carried to the lounge where the whole party gathered round him. "Seth, I think a prayer is in order," he quietly stated when the sobbing had sufficiently subsided.

The hardest, most inadequate prayer of my life followed, as the room fell silent. Policemen, coroner, nurse, cousins, all silent.

"... Amen."

I finished and looked up, but Clive, with head still bowed, began to pray, a prayer to the God who had taken his daughter with all her potential, to a better, more perfect place. His prayer reduced the nurse, the coroner and me to tears; even the policemen were clearly moved. Someone coughed; we stood up and once again we began the long walk along the basement corridor in silence.

James, the parish vicar looked concerned. "I'm sorry to say it, but I didn't know where to sit it was so dirty," he said. He'd just returned from Clive's house, having conducted the usual bereavement visit.

"James," I said. "You should've been there before they tidied up!"

"You're joking," he replied, disbelievingly.

"No, I'm only too serious. It's so hard for them with nine, sorry eight, people in one three-bedroomed house. It isn't really surprising that things get on top of them."

With the funeral only a few days away, the pressure had been mounting. No matter what we said to the residents of Bluebell Common, horrible rumours abounded and threats were issued against Clive and Barry. It was crunch time for Clive's new-found faith – he was in the crucible with the heat turned fully on; would he cope? He lost control at times, seeking solace from the bottom of a bottle, but on the whole, with the help of the church, he rode the stormy period up until the day of the funeral.

After Jane's passing, the family lurched from crisis to crisis, spiralling down to an incident with terrible consequences when the family was split up when their children were taken into care. We'll hear more about that later. The following few pages are the real thing, a transcript of an interview with Clive that was conducted in his house just a few months after his family were reunited by the courts. The report from the Area Child Protection Committee described the inter-agency work with Clive's family as a model case. From the church's point of view, it was nearly a model case. Four years on, Bea was worshipping with her children at the parish church, while Clive was a pillar of the Miners' Welfare Club, in the heart of the village that once ostracised him. Nothing has been taken out except the vocalisation of his daughter, who was learning how to speak.

Seth: I'm sat in Clive's house, talking about how we met. And perhaps some of this session might touch on some emotional areas. But really I wonder if you in your own words Clive could basically tell me how we first met?

Clive: Yeah... It wasn't on the best of terms we, we... we'd been robbed, we'd been robbed. You know that.

S: Yes. What had gone missing?

C: A tape recorder went missing, £75 in cash, two milk tokens, a TV. That were a rented TV. And when we found out who had done it, I were wanting to... I would have broken every bone in his body if it hadn't have been for you coming up.

S: So what happened? I knocked on the door and you opened the door.

C: I thought it were one of his goons.

S: Yes.

C: We know who we're on about now, John E. I thought it was one of his... I thought it were an henchman. And I turned round, I turned round to Bea and I said, who the bloody hell is this coming to the door. If we haven't had enough trouble, we've got this coming now.

S: What did you think was going to happen when I came?

C: So I didn't even bother waiting for you coming to the door. I went outside and I met you, I met you at the wall.

And were about to ask "who are you and what do you want."

S: You said you thought that I was one of John E.'s goons, henchmen, what did you think that I was coming to do then?

C: Personally kick seven barrels out of me. Tha' looked a damn sight bigger than me, still does.

S: But what happened that day?

C: It was, what you actually says to me was "I've come to appeal to your better nature." John E. was going through a bad time anyway, it were virtually the breaking point. He was going to try to commit suicide, I think that's what you said. And that you appealed to my better nature not to go around causing any more trouble. To think before I acted. Therefore I did. That was the first time I met you. I never thought any more of it. I wasn't even interested in church in religion or anything. And that were it for about four month, four or five month I think.

S: Apart from the odd kick of a football on the field.

C: Yeah, apart from the odd kick of a football, yeah.

S: Right, but even that meeting was perhaps dramatic enough wasn't it really?

C: Yes, yeah I don't think neither of us, I don't think neither of us would have known what to expect.

S: That's right, I think we were both as wary of each other as the other was. You know what I mean?

C: Yeah. I were more wary of you knowing what had gone off. I felt, I felt I were going… I felt anger. Now at the time I couldn't describe it, I wouldn't be able to describe that feeling. But I suppose even then I knew then that something must have been working in me. Something had appealed to me better nature and it wasn't just you.

S: Yeah, that's right. Now this anger ends up being quite an important thing in your life, doesn't it? Because it comes in time after time after time. Er and perhaps still now and then it rears its ugly head every now and then doesn't it.

C: It does, yeah.

S: But we seem to have got it licked with the help of the Lord, do we not?

C: We do have it licked.

S: Great... In those few months when I hardly ever saw you after that incident, something happened to you and Bea, you had a baby, a child, a young girl called Jane. But the thing was she wasn't delivered in the normal way like most people's babies are delivered at hospital. Can you explain a bit about it?

It is at this point that the tape recording becomes inaudible. The years have taken their toll and the rest of the interview is lost, but my memory and my diaries brought most of it back. These were my first converts. An achievement. Notches on my Bible cover, right?

Chapter 4

THE SOUND OF THE CROWD

Helping Clive and Bea pick up the pieces of their life after their children were taken into care cost me dearly, but more of that later. As the days following their bereavement merged into weeks, Clive began to drift away from the church and closer to the Miners' Welfare club. The more he drank the less he needed the crutch of the church. My contact with him lessened.

The death of little Jane was devastating, but what then happened to her sister was appalling.

I visited and saw the signs of inevitable decline. Eight people in a three-bedroomed house. Filth on the floor. Soiled nappies on the sofa. The tacky feeling of your shoes sticking to the carpet as you walked across the room. Things were definitely not getting better. I noticed the new fist-sized holes in the doors. Anger was residing in this house.

Barry now ruled the roost; Clive's response was to make himself scarce and lose himself in drink.

I visited the house with a carrier bag full of cans of beans, a couple of loaves, some milk and cereal. The previous day, when their benefit cheque arrived, Clive cashed it and drank the whole fortnight's finance in one session. 13 days to go before more money came along. Nothing I said could penetrate Clive's defences. He had succumbed to his old demons and they had brought their friends along with them for a party.

I was busy fending off questions about why they weren't in church, after all the help they had received from us. Much to my shame I was nursing resentment because my prize converts had fucked off. You see, despite what you might think, you need a trophy or two to display to the church, to the rich leafy-lane benefactors who supported our work, or they might begin to lose interest. Worse still, I might have lost face.

I told myself that it was all for the Kingdom of God, that I was worried for Clive's soul, for Bea's soul. Not exactly true. It was probably also for my benefit. That's why I kept a secret score of all those who bent the knee to the Lord Jesus and repeated the sinner's prayer after me. My boss, the minister, was asking why they didn't come to church much anymore. He was telling me I had to round up my errant flock and herd them there on Sunday mornings. I was feeling the familiar deflation as failure nipped at my heels.

I was pondering this and questioning my motives, while nursing a long cold cup of tea at home. My mood was pierced by A neighbour furiously rattling the windowpane. I shook my head to clear my thoughts and raced to the kitchen door. Flinging it open, I was confronted with Caz, a young single parent who lived over the alleyway from me.

"Seth you've got to come quickly. They've kicked in the gypos' door and are beating Clive and Barry up," she blurted out breathlessly.

"Hold on. Just a minute."

I gabbled whilst trying to make sense of what she had said. "The gypos" was how some of the villagers had started to refer to Clive and Barry and their respective families, as they slipped further and further into squalor and deprivation.

"Who's kicked the door in? And why?"

"A big gang of them. Hawley, Fish-eyes and some others."

"But why?" I asked again, as a feeling of dread began to take root and drain the courage from me: a feeling known to street fighters as 'bottle drop'. It happens when a charge of adrenaline is replaced by fear. It might have flattered my ego to think that Caz had such faith in me, but who was I to go and stop a group of young men intent on an act of extreme violence? I tapped my foot on the doorframe to try to disguise the trembling of my leg. There clearly wasn't enough time for me to telephone Marvin, the six-foot-six giant, to come and stand by my side. I had visited his mother as she slowly succumbed to cancer, and he repaid me with friendship and an occasional show of force when needed. His arrival on a motorbike that resembled a child's ride-on toy due to his ample frame had been all that was needed to cause a group of rowdy youths to disperse. There was no time to ring round and ask him to come. I was on my own.

"Just give me a minute."

I panicked as I sought to gain some control over my fear. I opened my under-sink cupboard, pulled out a hammer, a handful of nails, a bolt and a hasp.

"What are you going to do with that lot?" Caz exclaimed.

"Carpentry," I shouted, as I ran out of the door.

I jogged up the hill and even from 100 yards I could see a small group of people standing in Clive's yard.

"Oi, Seth. Are you going to the beasts' house," called John.

John was one of the young men who came to the youth club for an hour or so each weekday. We had some European funding to open the youth club for unemployed young people, a commodity we had no shortage of in our village.

"What do you mean beasts' house?" I asked.

"Don't you know what's gone on?" John enquired.

"No, I don't and I need to know quickly, before I get there," I snapped, losing patience.

"Folk are saying they've had a go at their own girls."

I stopped in my tracks.

Time out! I needed a reality check. Had I just heard what I thought I'd heard?

"You what? What did you say?" I asked.

"The police came and took all the kids away," he clarified. "Everyone says it's because they've had a go at their own girls. Stands to reason, doesn't it? I mean they did take the kids away."

Oh my God. The one unforgivable sin on Bluebell Common estate, and many like it, was child abuse. You could be a moneylender, you could demand money with menaces, you could be a burglar and still be accepted – welcomed even. A drug dealer was seen by some as just another service provider. If you were an armed robber you were treated with reverence and respect; street fighters were admired. But if you committed child sexual abuse, you were marked out as the lowest of the low. You were a beast or a nonce, and fair game. You were green lit, meaning anyone could have a go. More than that, it was considered your duty to have a go.

Just prior to my arrival, a father of a family just four doors down from me had allegedly broken one of his children's arms. I didn't know what had taken place. I made the mistake, in the eyes of the villagers, of calling round to visit.

I was curious because the windows of the bottom floor of the house had been bricked up. It was to all intents and purposes just another empty, abandoned property. And yet I'd seen people coming and going; did someone live there? As I entered the property, I was greeted by full-scale, abject poverty. No carpets on the floor, piles of rubbish scattered about the place, a single light bulb without a shade dangling from the ceiling. I refused the kind offer of a drink. The sink, I'd noticed as I entered through the kitchen, was piled high with foul, stained crockery. I asked why the windows were bricked up and was told it was because they were persecuted by the village children. A neighbour later explained what had happened, telling me that I should keep away. The father had supposedly rough-handled his daughter, breaking her arm, which led to the house being smashed up.

Child abuse. The unforgivable sin of the estate. If that was their reaction to physical abuse, how could I get involved when Clive and Barry were suspected of worse? And yet they'd no one else to turn to at that moment. I had to get involved, didn't I?

I was nearly at the house. I had to make a decision. Did I carry on and risk the wrath of the baying mob, or did I turn round and slink back to Church House and fester in a sea of regret and self-recrimination?

I knew that much of what I'd been told in the village had been embellished, misheard, misreported or just plain made up. It gave an insight into the accuracy of the oral tradition that led to the writing of many of the books of the Bible. As stories were repeated, they mutated, evolving into folklore that bore little resemblance to the original events.

The only information I had to go on was what I'd just been told. There was no actual proof that anything had happened. The kernel, the probable truth, was that the children had been taken away by the police and so the men had been beaten up.

If I sided with the family, I might become a target of the mob myself. And yet these men who were gathered at the end of the yard had made themselves judge, jury and executioner. Summary justice had been meted out, but did they have all the evidence to come to their conclusion?

This thought decided it for me. Nobody actually knew what had happened. There was no evidence of any abuse having taken place.

But here before me was evidence of an actual beating; a door had been smashed open and the wives were alone, frightened, threatened and in need of someone to support them.

Time to earn your pittance, I thought to myself, as I approached the house.

"Excuse me mate, coming through," I said as I made my way through the group of men standing at the end of the yard.

"What are you going in there for, Seth?" Fish-eyes called out to a murmur of approval. "They're nonces!"

I knew an answer was expected, but what could I say? I was stumped. I decided the best policy was to say nothing for the moment.

The door was unusable; it had been kicked in and the frame had splintered outwards where the lock was.

I didn't go any further; I didn't even know if anyone was in the house. I just started to do what I could. Taking the screws out of my pocket I began to screw the bolt and hasp into the door and frame. The house couldn't be locked if it was unoccupied, but at least it was some defence against people trying to get in. I turned my attention to the bottom panel where the door had been kicked in, and tried to patch it up as best I could with the piece of plywood I had brought with me.

The mob was growing agitated, I could hear snatches of "beasts", "nonces" and "need to be taught a lesson".

"I said…" Fish-eyes shouted louder with venom in his voice. I stood up, hammer still in my hand, and looked at him. His real name was Simon, but because of his bulging eyes, everybody knew him as Fish-eyes. He was well over six feet tall, and I was under five foot ten. He was powerfully built and seemed to be ready for action, but I had a hammer in my hand. He was bouncing up and down on his toes, one hand was balled into a fist by his side and the other was pointing in my direction, jabbing to emphasise his words, "…you shouldn't be fucking well helping them. They're beasts. We got Barry and we're waiting for Clive. He's got it coming." He spoke almost proudly and clearly had the approval of the crowd.

"Does anybody here know what happened?" I asked, looking around the mob from one face to another. It was important that I made them feel like individuals, not part of a mob. I wanted them to think for themselves and not be carried by a collective emotional tide.

"Who knows what happened?"

I was pretty sure that nobody would've talked to the police, for fear of being labelled a grass. Any information they'd gained would be suspect to say the least.

"You say they're beasts, Fish-eyes; how do you know?" I asked.

Fish-eyes was clearly the appointed spokesperson.

"The pigs took the kids away. I heard them say it was abuse," he said, with authority.

"Let's say that you heard right," I said, with a conviction I didn't really feel. "Who's to say that it was Clive or Barry that did it, that is if anything actually happened?"

I was on a roll now, warming to my theme and gesturing with my hammer.

"I mean, Fish-eyes, I've seen *you* in that house. Doddy," I said, pointing out a skinny youth. "I've seen *you* in that house, too. Even if something happened, we don't know the facts of it yet. We don't know who did what."

With that, I bent down, turned to the door and continued to nail the panel in place.

I didn't look up until the job was done. When I did, I got a surprise. There was no longer a crowd at the end of the drive. They had melted away in ones and twos, and I was on my own.

Clive never did get his. He escaped street justice. What followed was some of the most intensive inter-agency cooperation I had ever been part of. We never did find out who had abused the child. By 'we' I mean me and the senior case worker, a child protection officer for Social Services. We had our suspicions, but these didn't rest on Clive or Barry. The next eight months of my working life can be summed up in this extract from a reference the case worker wrote for me.

> Seth is known to have gained respect within the community by the way he has communicated with residents, given practical and counselling support to families and individuals. For example, with one particular family, Seth has given ongoing support in conjunction with Social Services staff. He has assisted the parents in finding babysitters to enable the father to attend vocational night-school classes whilst the wife attends adult learning classes. Seth has encouraged the father to take greater responsibility within his family. To assist the parents in their attempts to keep the children out of local authority care, Seth was instrumental in getting financial assistance through the auspices of the church. This money was used to pay off debts so that the weekly income was then made available for present living expenses. When the parents were involved in care proceedings at court,

Seth accompanied them and gave them support throughout their ordeal.

With other families in Bluebell Common, Seth Walker has given counselling support to parents, involved the teenage children in church activities and encouraged neighbours to develop active involvement with one another. He has always responded to the social workers' concerns about individuals and families in the community, monitoring and liaising with us wherever appropriate.

I rediscovered these words 28 years after they were written. I found it hard to recognise myself. However, each line sparked memories. Of sitting as a team at the family meeting when the professionals agreed that Barry was to be told he had to leave the house, along with his wife and two children, so that Clive had a chance to rebuild his family. It seemed a good course of action; however, Barry's criminal record and history of violence meant they were wary of telling him.

It fell to me to have that difficult conversation. I felt sick to the stomach with fear and anxiety for what would become of Barry and his little family, but it had to be done; the decision was already made, and I would rather it came from me. I watched on, ashamed, as Barry and his family packed their belongings into duvet covers and bin bags and left by taxi for bed and breakfast accommodation. Not a fairytale ending by any stretch of the imagination.

I remember taking Clive to pick out wallpaper and paint for his little girl's room. When he proudly showed me his handywork, I noted, but didn't point out, that he'd hung the rainbow wallpaper upside down. Overall, I think the letter from the social worker was right; this was a piece of good work that changed lives for the better.

My ministry was helping me to develop as a person, and every time I saw Clive and his family at Church House, I knew that a little light can shine even in the darkest of lives.

Chapter 5

YEAH RIGHT

Barry was on a journey, as we all are, but for a short time, it seemed to me that he was making his way into the family of the church at Bluebell Common. As the turmoil at home waxed and waned, Barry had made his decision to become a Christian, to bow the knee and say the sinner's prayer. However, in the crucible of real life, that faith was tested. Was it found wanting? Did it ever take root and grow into something life changing and beautiful? I'll let you decide.

I spent quite some time with Barry, between Clive's daughter dying and children being taken into care. This is his story as recounted to me. The account is as close to his words as possible, and in wanting to convey them, I am not implying any endorsement of their veracity. I will leave you to make up your own mind as to its authenticity.

Barry, like many of you, was christened as a baby. The church sees this as the child being welcomed into the community of faith, but he was never brought up in the family of the church. His parents were not church goers, so he hadn't known who Jesus was or been taught to love him. The only time he prayed or even sang a hymn was at school, during assembly. As a young pupil, he began to play truant from religious observances and hide in the toilets. He began to feel a resentment towards God that grew and grew until he decided to turn his back on Christ. Some would argue that this process was far from usual and would therefore have unusual consequences.

He recalls beginning to get into trouble when he was nine years old; just petty crimes at first, like shoplifting, progressing to breaking into cars and sheds, then becoming more serious: burgling houses or warehouses. It was a steep progression and he seemed to have a talent for sin that he described as being "Given by the devil". He used language that implied a process was taken place that was beyond his control. It was as if he was a pawn in a game and not responsible for his actions. For example, he told me that the worst ability he received was violence, and it would plague him for many years to come.

At the time our paths crossed, he thought that his faith had enabled him to control his violence; for a time, that seemed to be the case. "Praise God," he once said, "it's nowhere near as powerful as it was and with Jesus's help, I'm able to keep it in check."

However, as a younger man, he sometimes couldn't control his violence, and this led to what he described as a bad mistake that took him on a dark journey. Even though they weren't church goers, his anger became so extreme that his parents, desperate and in the absence of any other explanation, thought that a demon had possessed him. He told me that on one awful occasion he blackened his mother's eyes when he lost control of himself in an argument. His dad called the police and they locked him up overnight for the first time.

There then followed a long series of incidents, culminating in a sickening attack when he'd been drinking. He and a group of mates went out to a bar which was known as a social venue for people with alternative lifestyles. People hid who they were in the ignorance of those times, and were unable to be open about their relationships and express their love and sexuality. Over 30 years ago, intolerance bred hate, finding expression in repellent violence. They'd waited outside the bar, and after about half an hour a man came out. They followed him. As he walked down a side street, they attacked him and beat him up. Some of them were satisfied with knocking him off his feet, but not Barry. He lost it completely and kept hitting him over and over again. They had to drag him off; the mist had descended and he was out of control. When he came to, he didn't really know what he'd done or why he'd done it. The narrative I was hearing was "The devil made me do it." I didn't buy it then, and I don't buy it now. When he got home the police were already there; someone had grassed on him, he recalled. Notice the language: he emphasised that he was the victim; he stressed that a low-down informer had done the wrong thing, not that he'd committed a shocking and violent assault and was now rightly to face justice. He was arrested and charged with Actual Bodily Harm. The innocent victim was so badly beaten that his nose and chin were broken, amongst other injuries.

When he got back from the police station on bail, his parents had reached the end of their meagre remaining supply of tolerance. Familiar bonds were strained to breaking point. They locked him out of the house, telling him never to darken their door again.

He lived rough for about a month but realised this was no way to carry on. He had to catch a break, to make a change, so he decided to join the Army. He contacted his parents, and a limited reconciliation was brokered. They liked the changes he was making, and things were looking up. During his brief time in the Army, he had his first real experience of Christianity, but only because he was compelled to go to chapel by a superior. On his first leave he met Lisa Marie; he seemed to catch her eye with his swagger and new-found fitness. He was smitten and wanted her more than anything else in his life. He spent as much of that week with her as he could. Leave finished all too soon and he returned to camp, writing to her nearly every day and thinking about her all the time. He used each weekend pass to spend precious time with her. With only 12 weeks of basic training left he had a decision to make: to leave and be with Lisa Marie or stay on. It was no contest and he asked to be discharged. He would rather have fun with Lisa Marie than have an officer telling him what to do and when to do it.

Life for the young couple started to move at a pace; he got a job and they moved into a flat. Things were looking up and life was full of promise. As time went on, they became sure they wanted to get married, but Lisa Marie's dad wasn't convinced. Barry's reputation may have proceeded him, and he was unable to obtain her parent's permission. They made a life-changing decision, one that you may consider far from wise. If he got Lisa Marie pregnant, then her dad couldn't stop them. It worked; six months later they were married, and three months after that they had a baby son. Things seemed to be going great. He had a lovely wife, a beautiful baby son and a steady job.

In an instant, though, his life started to come apart at the seams. He lost his job, through no fault of his own, he said. Shortly afterwards, his son became seriously ill and was rushed to hospital where he was put in an oxygen tent and treated for nearly a month. That was the first time he can remember that he turned to the Lord, asking him to help his son every night. He bowed his knee in the hospital chapel and made promises, pledging his life to God if only his son would recover. But when he did, Barry never even went near a church. His promises were hollow and quickly forgotten.

The next few paragraphs are very hard for me to write, but again, I am recalling the account as closely to his telling as possible. I feel angry about this as a process, but if I don't capture it this way, we'll lose sight of what the narrative tells us. Leaping out from these words are stark warnings to avoid self-deception and not to abdicate responsibility for your own actions. Most tragically, the belittling of domestic abuse and its traumatic impact on women and developing young children is heart breaking.

It was soon after this that life got even worse. He couldn't get a job; it was the 1980s and recession had hit England. After being rejected several times, he started to drink. It wasn't long before his anger bubbled up and the violence with it; he started to hit Lisa Marie about. He was lazy around the house and day by day the situation was getting worse and worse. When Lisa Marie told him she was pregnant again, there was no joy this time. It was unbearable; he had no job, and they could only just afford to live as things were – how could they manage with another mouth to feed?

For a while, circumstances changed for the better. He managed to get a job again and life began to get back to how it used to be. He kept his fists down, but 12 months later the drinking and the violence came back.

Lisa Marie had seen enough of him and his ways. She left him to live with a neighbour, who he thought was a mate. The betrayal hit him hard; he felt like murdering him at first, but the neighbour had a shady past and a bad reputation. Heartbroken, he went into shock, shut down and took an overdose. His cousin, who lived up the street, heard that Lisa Marie had gone and came round about midnight to check in on him. He saw that he was unconscious and called an ambulance. Barry woke up around six the next morning in hospital. He had a strange feeling that someone was looking over him, and that feeling stayed with him for a long time. But who was it? He wasn't sure. When he was discharged he was sent to stay with his parents, to look after him and probably to make sure he wouldn't do it again.

When he recovered, he started moping around the house; he couldn't stop crying. He wished Lisa Marie would come back. He was bored and was looking through some books when he came across a Bible. He blew the dust off and started reading. When the words hit home and spoke to him about his situation, he started to pray. From then on, when he prayed, Barry would promise his life to God if he would get Lisa Marie back and help him out of this mess. He joined the empty-promise club that so many others rushed to be a part of when facing a crisis. Membership is usually short, coinciding with the crisis coming to an end. His actions in calling out to God in times of trouble will be familiar to many. He was convinced that he was serious this time; he meant what he prayed and felt funny inside, a kind of peaceful feeling. Within a month his prayers were answered at last: Lisa Marie and the kids returned. They left their old house, making themselves voluntarily homeless, and Barry swore he would never go back to the same village ever again. The only housing they were offered was bed and breakfast accommodation. It was tough going.

However, Barry again failed to keep his promise to the Lord, living his life for himself and not for God. He still prayed sometimes, and he always reminded himself of the promise he'd made to follow Jesus. Six months of bed and breakfast living was all this family of four could stand. They upped and left. With nowhere else on offer, they had no alternative but to go to his cousin who lived in the village he'd vowed never to return to. He didn't want to go back but felt that a strange power was taking him there. He suggested this power was God; it was the power of the Lord that took him back to Bluebell Common because it was there that he met the man who lived in Church House, Seth. Our paths crossed through a daytime provision for unemployed young adults. We worked out, played sport and talked. As his life story came out, I kept on at him to come to church. He always made an excuse or outright refused, until one day I wouldn't take no for an answer. Insisting, I took him to a meeting. He only intended to go to please me, but once there all he could do was listen to the preacher, a converted street fighter with a story that Barry could relate to. All the time he was speaking, Barry was thinking of his promise to the Lord and then everything started to make sense.

The next thing he knew, as the preacher called people forward to repent, he was walking up to the front, unaware of anyone or anything. He committed himself to God. He describes it as a significant event. From that day on he never looked back, other than to thank God for saving his son and his marriage. He had become convinced that the person looking over him when he took the overdose must've been the Lord, and that funny feeling inside must've been the power of the Holy Spirit working within him.

Since becoming a Christian, he describes life as having new meaning; his body feels more alive, as though the Lord has given him new eyes to see and new ears to hear his word. He wanted to shout it from the highest mountain. He'd been given a new purpose in life, a goal to aim for. It feels as though the Lord has come down and breathed fresh air into his lungs and given him a chance to begin again. Before, he was always hungry for a fight; now he's hungry only for the word of God and always wants to please and serve God rather than himself. When he became a Christian, he lost a few friends, but gained a family: the family of God. Becoming a Christian is hard, but staying a Christian is even harder. He has learnt that. He has found a new and better life loving Jesus who died for our sins, and he still loves every one of us. This is his story of a journey on the road to Christianity; it may be a hard and rocky one, but it's one with a solid foundation on which to build.

Yeah, right.

I'm sipping a nice malt whisky and reading this account, over 30 years on, with a sense of sadness and cynicism. During the time I knew Barry, I'm not convinced he ever really changed. Desperation that took him to the lost world of Bluebell Common and desperation would take him out of it. Previously, he had his own council house in the village, along with his own wife and children. Although it wasn't perfect, it had all the ingredients of what could have been a satisfying and even rewarding life. However, all this changed when he discovered his wife had fallen for the charms of a neighbour. This man was described to me as a violent ex-Hells Angel. I never found out whether he used to be an outlaw biker, but his supposed propensity for violence was soon to be directed towards me. I'm convinced this was a consequence of helping Barry and his family.

Barry had managed to win his wife's affection back, but when the ex-biker heard this, he paid Barry a visit. He meted out a significant beating, then smashed all the windows on the ground floor of the house he was renting from the council.

That's why Barry, his wife and two children fled, and sought refuge at Clive's house in Bluebell Common. They moved into the tiny three-bedroomed terraced house, already the home of two adults and two children.

The decision had been taken during a 'team around the family' meeting with social workers and health visitors.

Barry and his family should move out. No one knew who had committed the awful offence that resulted in Clive's children being taken away, but the social workers were adamant that the living conditions had contributed to the abuse. Barry had undermined Clive in his own house, and there was no chance of rebuilding the family and re-establishing effective parenting, with eight people in a three-bedroomed terraced house.

There was a reluctance from those present to approach Barry to tell him what was going to have to happen. His criminal record, including his violent offences, was brought up. However, I had worked out and played football alongside him and knew that he probably wouldn't present a physical threat. I also knew that he committed Actual Bodily Harm as part of a gang, against one defenseless person.

When I visited him to tell him he'd have to leave Clive's house, it soon became apparent that any talk of following God meant nothing to him. I faced the brunt of his anger; perhaps some of it was deserved – hadn't I told him that with Christ in the vessel we can smile at the storm?

Watching someone stuff their meager belongings into duvet covers, pillowcases and black bin bags is not a pleasurable experience. Knowing that Barry was heading to bed-and-breakfast accommodation with his wife and two children was a bitter pill to swallow. I thought back to an Ethics lecture two years previously, when we'd told we'd often be called upon to make decisions which would lead to neither a good or bad outcome, but we would sometimes have to choose between the lesser of two evils.

I was here, not in the cloistered halls of academia discussing hypothetical situations, but in the real world, favouring one family over another. Was it a good choice? I don't know. Did I have the right to make it? Probably not, but something had to happen. My dad has some interesting mottos that he would recite to me at times. He told me that when he was being admonished for getting something wrong, his response was, "I prefer the way I did it to the way you didn't." That seemed apt in this case. My actions and my decisions may not have been the best, but I was there when no one else was and I did what little I could to make a difference.

Chapter 6

CLIVE AND THE PIT

Have you ever witnessed a flood?

I have, in my village, nestled in the foothills of the Pennines, during an autumn storm. A branch had fallen into a brook and blocked a culvert. As the rain fell on the hillside, the water pressure built up behind a wall until it was breached, and the raging waters carried a tumbling mass of debris into the centre of the village. The burst seemed to come out of nowhere and was out of proportion to the rainfall. The blockage caused the build-up, which in turn led to the chaos and damage.

As the months passed, Clive increasingly immersed himself in his college course; his little family had been saved and he wasn't going to let anything split them up again. However, something was blocking Clive's wellbeing. He hadn't channelled his emotions in a healthy way and the pressures were building.

When I called to see him he was clearly angry. So much so, I was worried that his anger might turn to violence. It was clear that something was welling up in him, but he wasn't telling me what.

I suggested that he come with me down to Church House and have a chat over a cup of tea. His children were playing noisily, and I thought there was more chance of him opening up if he was on his own.

Once there, I put the kettle on.

"Okay Clive, what's been eating you?" I enquired as I sat opposite him.

He viewed me through narrow eyes and eventually admitted, "It's that there Billy, he keeps calling me a beast." His head drooped forward. "I can't do anything about it, because if I say owt, he'll kick seven barrels out of me."

When Clive's children had been taken into care, it was devastating for all those involved but particularly hard for him. He knew he hadn't been involved in any kind of abuse, neither had his wife. And yet he felt that he'd been punished by losing his children.

He knew that his cousin and himself were the chief suspects as far as the villagers were concerned. Imagine the pain you would feel if you were being blamed for such a heinous crime, of which you were innocent, committed against one of your own children. If that wasn't bad enough, he also carried the terrible guilt that he'd let the abuser into his house and left him with his children. We had spent many hours talking, building him up to enable him to be emotionally ready to face the family court and eventually to regain custody of his own children.

I had raised nearly £1,500, a considerable sum 30 years ago, to settle the family's debts, buy them some new furniture and purchase some home decoration supplies.

The work we did with the family, alongside the health visitors, Social Services and a secure children's centre run by an angel in human form, remains the most significant I've ever been involved in.

After months of hard work, counselling and court appearances, the family had been reunited, and Clive had thrown himself into his studies. He hoped that with some qualifications to show employers, he would be able to get a job and begin to provide for his family.

However, all this progress was being undermined by Billy's taunts. Every time Billy called out "Beast!" Clive found himself angry and frustrated. He knew he wasn't a beast and had done everything in his power to give his family a second chance. But here was Billy chipping away at his resolve, his confidence and self-esteem. Clive knew he couldn't stop the taunts. Each time he heard the cry, old wounds would reopen that went all the way back to his childhood, and he'd be reminded of how he'd let his daughter down by not protecting her. He knew that by withdrawing from his family responsibilities all those months ago, and seeking solace in drink, he'd created the conditions that had allowed the abuser to strike.

I was at a loss what to say, or how to move the situation on. However, I did have one advantage over Clive, in that I had some leverage with Billy. I had seen Billy at his most vulnerable and had been there for him at his lowest point, when Billy had decided that he had nothing to live for, and nearly made a choice which would have seen him locked up for life. I'd been able to stop that happening, and now I felt that he owed me.

"Clive, the next time Billy calls you a beast, I want you to say to him that Seth wants you to stop saying that. Tell him that if he won't, I'll come and see him to talk about it."

Clive lifted his head and furrowed his brow as he pondered what I'd said.

"You what?" He expressed his disbelief at what I had just said. "You really think that will stop him?"

As he spoke, each word grew louder and louder until he was shouting. He suddenly rocked onto his feet and stood up. He was clearly worked up; I felt at a disadvantage being seated, but didn't want to stand up in case he saw it as a provocation. He was in the grip of fury and losing control of himself. His arms wind-milled with empty punches.

"Call me a fucking beast will you?" he called out to the absent Billy. "I'll show you who's a beast."

He was getting louder and inching closer to me.

This was completely bizarre. It seemed out of all proportion to what I'd just said, and there was clearly more to the situation than met the eye. I think that Billy's taunts had not only knocked the scab off old wounds, but had tapped into something deeper and darker that was blighting Clive's life. Something had caused him to lock away a deep-seated hurt, which had festered as resentments grew. Recent events coupled with the taunting had caused these resentments to swell and the pressure to build; the walls had now been breached and all the years of hurt and hate were flooding out in a torrent of emotion.

It was reaching such a pitch that I was beginning to worry for my safety. I moved to my left, to dodge Clive's flailing arms, stood up and took a step back from him.

"Clive, Clive!"

I desperately tried to get his attention.

"Clive!"

But he was oblivious to me. I realised this wasn't an attempt to attack me, but his fury was venting in any and every direction. As he shouted, his words lost their form and broke down into guttural utterances and choking grunts. His flailing subsided and his hands reached for his throat. He appeared to be choking. As feral, animalistic sounds emerged, he looked as if he was having difficulty removing an object from his gullet. It was utterly terrifying. He sagged down to his knees, as I looked on incredulous, not knowing what to do.

"Clive, are you alright Clive?" I panicked as I reached out to shake him by his shoulder. At my touch, he fell forward on to the floor and began to writhe, his body moving from side to side in an undulating, serpentine fashion. The choking noises had gone, and in place was a rasping hiss. He looked up at me from slitted eyes and his tongue shot in and out of his mouth.

I was gripped with a sense of primitive, primal panic. I felt as if I was in the presence of something alien, alien and ancient. I was overwhelmed, at a loss what to do, and I'd nothing to offer other than, "Clive, you've got to call on the name of Jesus! You've got to call on the name of Jesus to save you."

Clive seemed completely oblivious to what I had to say. He continued to writhe as I started to pray. With each prayer, I regained a little more control of myself. My fear was subsiding. I decided that I needed to take authority over whatever was plaguing Clive, so I claimed victory by the power of the blood of Jesus. I commanded any unclean spirits to leave and go to the place appointed for them.

Clive's animalistic movements slowed down and it seemed as if he was regaining some measure of control.

"Come on Clive, call on the name of Jesus!" I implored. "Clive, say Jesus!"

He started to struggle to gain control of his voice.

"J… J… Je… Jes… Jes…" he stuttered and hissed.

"Jesus!" He managed to form the word, and then he repeated, "Jesus, Jesus, Jesus!"

It appeared as if Clive was becoming more aware of himself and his surroundings. He pushed himself to his knees, looked up at me and tried to stand up. I caught hold of him beneath his arms and guided him to the sofa. He looked bewildered, gazing at the floor and then at me.

"How the bloody hell did I get down there?" were the first words he uttered to me after regaining control.

"One minute we were talking and the next you were shouting and angry," I began to explain. "And then you were on the floor. Do you know what was happening to you?" I asked, breathing heavily with relief.

"All I can describe it as, it was like being pulled down into a dark, deep, stinking pit. I didn't think I was going to get out," he said in disbelief.

"What was it that pulled you out?" I enquired.

"It was saying the name of Jesus," he offered.

Looking back now as a skeptic and an atheist, I've found it hard to rationalise some of what took place in that room on that day. But it has real meaning for me and serves as a powerful warning to never bottle up, gloss over or hide those hurts and resentments that life gifts us over the years. In doing so we might be damming up a lake of pain, that one day might come flooding out with devastating consequences.

Billy did call Clive a beast again, but only once. Clive recited the reply I had given to him. Billy told Clive that he wasn't scared of Seth. However, he never taunted him again, and Clive could walk the streets with his head held high once again.

Chapter 7

SUICIDAL AMBITION

I had just 30 minutes to gather my notes and make my way up to the parish church, which was two miles away. I planned on walking for the sake of the exercise. I would have to jog a little if I was going to be there on time. It was my turn to lead the mid-week parish Bible study and I knew that the churchwardens would have already opened up and prepared the small side chapel. I picked up my Bible along with my notes and headed towards the kitchen. As I opened the door, I was surprised to be greeted by Sarah Jayne, her arm raised, as if she was ready to knock on the door.

Sarah Jayne was Clive's niece by marriage; her mother, Jean, lived over the road and was a frequent visitor to that chaotic household. Years of drug and alcohol misuse had taken their toll on Jean; she was a frail shell of a human being. She had recently re-dedicated her life to the Lord and had told me about her early teenage years. She left home to avoid abuse and fell in love with a biker. She described being part of an outlaw motorcycle club, called Black Sabbath, after the band, and were based in Leicester.

Although I'm familiar with the outlaw biker scene, I had never heard that particular gang mentioned before. The significant outfit in the area at that time were known as the 'Ratae MC' and had some links to the most established outlaw motorcycle clubs. I did know that trouble seemed to follow Jean around. However, her door was always open to her children and their families.

"Hey up Sarah Jayne are you alright?" I greeted.

If Sarah Jayne was knocking on my door, the chances were that she was almost certainly not alright. She might be penniless, and asking for money or food, but more likely there was trouble over the road.

"Seth, Mum wants to know if you can come over to hers," she jabbered, clearly anxious.

"Sorry Sarah Jayne," I answered. "I'm on my way out now, can't it wait?"

"You've got to come now. We need you. Carl is swallowing screws and popping his epilepsy pills."

Here we go again, I thought, as I locked my door and crossed the road.

"Oh, thank the Lord you've come," Jean said, as I entered the lounge.

Her son, Carl, was sat on the floor with his back against

an armchair. He was a skinhead, jeans turned up at the bottom to show off his Doc Marten boots. The short sleeves of his Fred Perry polo shirt showed his sinewy arms, decorated with long scars – he was an aficionado of self-harm before it became mainstream. The crisscrosses of small cuts bisected his many tattoos, some homemade and clumsily inked.

As I took the scene in, he met my gaze, smiled and stuck out his tongue. Not a quick gesture, like a child, but a deliberate one. His tongue remained out as he looked at me. Before I could react, he placed the ring pull of a beer can on his tongue. Retracting it into his mouth, he took a swig of supermarket own-brand special brew and swallowed it down.

I had met Carl before, briefly and in passing. He'd seemed to be trouble then, but this was on another level.

Smacking his lips, he said, "Ahhhh. That hits the fucking spot." He seemed proud of what he'd done.

"That's enough of that language, not in front of Seth anyway." Jean shot a gaze at him. "You see what he's like, Seth? He's been swallowing screws and taken his epilepsy pills. I'm worried he's going to kill himself."

"I want to be dead anyway," he declared. "Take me to the cells at Bradley and let me swing like our Kevin!"

This sounded like the drunken, drugged ramblings of a madman, but I knew only too well that there was something more sinister behind this utterance. Jean had previously told me that several years ago, Carl's older brother had been arrested and taken to Bradley Police Station. He'd been arrested on suspicion of rape, the rape of a pensioner. He never stood trial, so guilt or innocence was never established. According to Jean, the custody officers had taken his shoelaces from him but left him with his belt. During a routine inspection, he was found hanging from the window bars by his belt and died despite attempts to revive him. Carl had declared that he had one ambition in life: he intended to get himself arrested and banged up in Bradley cells, so he too could hang himself and join his brother.

As I sit here writing this memoir, nearly 30 years on, I'm struck by how ridiculous this sounds. And yet for me, as bizarre as this episode seems, it was real to all of us involved.

Carl, a real person, broken, damaged and probably fatally flawed, was a human being in need. What should I do?

Not for the last time, I faced a dilemma, the trading off of immediate need with prior commitment. I took a moment to think it through. Was I qualified and experienced enough to deal with Carl? The answer was a resounding no. Did my degree in Theology and Philosophy sufficiently qualify me to lead the parish Bible study? The answer was a resounding yes.

I motioned for Jean to follow me and we headed out towards the back door.

"Jean, I can't help here. Carl needs specialist medical help," I reasoned.

"You can't go, Seth. Don't leave us alone with him in this state, you don't know what he's like," she pleaded.

I reached out to put my hands on her bony shoulders.

"Jean, I'm not deserting you, but I can't help him, it's beyond me, and I'm due elsewhere." I started to build my argument. "You need to call 999 and get an ambulance here as soon as possible. He's been swallowing sharp objects and has taken an overdose of pills. You don't need a churchman to help you, you need a doctor." I sighed. "I've got to go, I'm due at Bible study for the next hour. I'll rush straight back."

It was no longer feasible to walk to the parish church. I drove on automatic pilot, thinking about Carl and Jean, of what would be going on back at Bluebell Common.

Perhaps my commitment to the prior-arranged Bible study was a powerful message in itself. Life in Bluebell Common was often governed by what was happening in the moment; a reactive existence, with no thought-out long-term plan or routine. People drifted, finding themselves reacting to the day-to-day circumstances of life, being driven like a rudderless boat in a storm.

My role was to establish routine, purpose, to demonstrate that if we put our hand to the rudder and steered our own course, we need not be victims of the circumstances of life. Or maybe I was fooling myself and trying to justify going to a Bible study with 11 parishioners while someone's life was in the balance. Not for the first time I was questioning myself and my motives.

Was I leaving these people in their time of need, because I was more worried about what the people in my church family would think if I didn't turn up to Bible study? Do you ever question your motives? Do you ever wonder whether you're doing the right thing? 30 years of adult life experience haven't provided me with any answers, and as I review my diary and look at my notes, I still don't know whether I did the right thing.

As soon as the Bible study session had finished, I made my apologies, and left. I told my story to a churchwarden and asked them to pray that I might be able to help in some way.

As I pulled up outside Church House, Sarah Jayne came running from across the road and accosted me as I climbed out of my car.

"Seth, we did what you said and called an ambulance," she blurted out.

"Good," I replied.

"No it fucking wasn't."

Her reply stung like a smack in the face.

"You should've stayed," she spat accusingly.

I was lost for words.

"When he saw the blue lights on the ambulance, he thought it was the police. He ran outside with a milk bottle."

"What?" I exclaimed, trying to understand what had happened.

"He ran into the field. He's pissed. He thought he was running away from the police," she continued. "The ambulancemen followed him, trying to get him to come to hospital. He thought they were the police and shouted at them to stay back. They didn't. So he smashed the bottle on a rock and held it to his throat. When they tried to move forward he slashed his wrist."

She'd started to sob. I was crestfallen; I'd made the wrong choice and let them down.

"They rushed him and we managed to get him into the ambulance and they took him away. They only left about 10 minutes ago." She shook her head. "You should have talked to him, Seth."

Her words were like a knife to my heart. Of course I should have stayed. Here was an immediate need, a pathetic, bruised, broken person and I'd left them to demonstrate my superior knowledge of scripture to my parishioners. What a fraud I was.

Without saying another word I walked across the road, got back in my car and headed towards the infirmary.

Tears were falling onto my lap as I drove. This was too much for me. After all, I was only 25 years old. This was my first post in a parish. How could anyone expect me to make good choices all the time? Why me? Self-pity is never a good thing. I wasn't even crying for Carl, but because of my bad decision-making, because of the look I got from Sarah Jayne and those words: "You should have stayed, Seth."

I didn't know why I was driving towards the hospital. I hadn't made a conscious decision but something inside me was calling the shots. 10 minutes later I pulled into the car park.

As I walked towards A&E, I again bemoaned the lack of a dog collar: that little strip of white plastic in the centre of the neck of a black collarless shirt opened doors, fast, and with very few questions asked.

I headed towards reception where Carl was at the centre of a commotion.

"Where's the fucking stairs?" he was calling out forcibly.

"Over here, Carl," I shouted as I beckoned to him. "I'll show you."

Several people in different uniforms were surrounding Carl, trying to corral him back towards the triage cubicles in A&E.

My aim was to walk him towards the treatment area and try to get some help for him. His left arm was badly gashed and blood was dripping onto the floor beside him.

"Come on, Carl, I'll show you," I called, with a confidence I didn't feel.

He did follow me, however, and the nurses parted to let him through. As I walked down the corridors hoping to loop back on myself, to head back towards A&E, I asked, "Why do you want to know where the stairs are, Carl?"

"Because I want to go up to the roof and jump off," he replied, matter-of-factly.

I knew I was in for a fight. This was not going to be easy. Carl wanted to die, and he was in a hospital full of drugs, sharp instruments and with a high roof. The odds were stacked in his favour. If he really wanted to do it, then the means to do so were everywhere.

After what seemed like an age of gentle walking, small talk, distraction and coercion, I managed to maneuver Carl into a cubicle. I was now spattered with his blood, and a blood trail marked our meandering passage through the corridors of the hospital.

A young doctor pulled back the curtain of the cubicle and had clearly decided to approach the situation with speed and decisive action.

"Let's have a look at this arm of yours," he said with authority.

Unbelievably, Carl held up his left arm and rested it on the gurney. A deep vertical gash ran for around seven inches from below the crook of his elbow towards his wrist. Semi-coagulated blood oozed from the open wound; elsewhere, dried blood was flaking off and falling like red dandruff.

"Right then, that's going to need a stitch or two," the doctor said. *And the rest*, I thought, as I looked at the gaping wound.

The doctor touched the tip of Carl's fingers and asked, "Can you feel that?"

I guessed he could, as Carl didn't answer verbally but instead launched a punch which glanced off the top of the doctor's head. Fortunately it didn't carry much force, as the doctor was standing while Carl was seated. Knowing Carl's state of mind, I stood between them and grabbed hold of Carl, doing my best to avoid his cut arm, making sure he couldn't get up.

The doctor fought to regain his composure. "That's enough of that, young man. I can't treat you if that's the way you're going to behave. You can wait there."

He made a hurried exit.

I felt like asking Carl why he'd done that. However, sometimes "least said soonest mended" is a good maxim to go by.

Just a few seconds later, the curtain was thrown back to reveal two large men wearing staff badges but no uniform. They walked in and both rested a hand on Carl's shoulders. Unbeknownst to me, the staff nurse had already phoned the psychiatric ward, and two experienced male nurses had been sent for. They arrived to see the doctor leaving the cubicle and heard his story before they hurried in.

"Now who's been a naughty boy then?" one of them said.

The other pointed at me and said, "You can wait outside."

He spoke with such authority I didn't even think to question him. Within half an hour, Carl was prepped and had entered an operating theatre, where his damaged arm would be repaired. However, it'd be a while before he would be discharged, as that evening he was sectioned under the mental health act.

Apart from a couple of short visits to the psychiatric ward, I saw very little of Carl after that. I found out from Jean that he'd made a good recovery, and, when he remembered to take his pills, he was alright. When he forgot, life around him was interesting.

I saw him again some months later. The council were on phase three of improving the houses in Bluebell Common. When the workmen left for the night, feral scavengers would move in to help themselves to anything that could be sold or could be useful to them. I saw Carl walking out of one of the houses carrying a new internal door on his back.

"Hello Carl," I called out. "What you got there?"

"Firewood," Carl replied with a grin and disappeared into the night.

Perhaps some light did manage to shine into his troubled life. Certainly, his medication kept him on an even keel.

That was the last I'd see of him. Thankfully, as far as I know, Carl hasn't fulfilled his ambition to kill himself and never will. Bradley Police Station was sold off and is now a private home. There are no cells left for him to visit.

Chapter 8

YOU'RE IN MY SOUL

It was late afternoon one August Bank Holiday Monday. I was exhausted after a weekend of safe partying at a Christian arts festival. I always enjoyed the relaxed atmosphere, the music and the meeting with friends, some of whom I wouldn't see for another 12 months. Now I had to settle my sleep debt! Borrowed tents had been dropped off with friends and the car parked in the alleyway next to Church House. The washing machine was straining to deal with the first load of muddy clothes when I heard an angry "bang, bang, bang!" from the alleyway. Looking out the kitchen window I saw a scrawny bespectacled youth jumping on the roof of my ageing car.

Young Kelvin seemed to spend an inordinate amount of time on my car roof, my kitchen roof, or, when he was feeling adventurous, on the actual roof of my house. Experience had taught me that shouting was the worst thing I could do.

Calling the police was totally out of the question because it would break the code of Bluebell Common. No one wanted to be known as a grass on our estate. At the very least, you would be branded as an outcast, a pariah, and you could expect your windows to be fair game for target practice. Or you might find yourself on the receiving end of a beating: summary justice, delivered from a warped sense of values. So I reached under the sink into the cupboard for an old Spiderman comic, opened the kitchen door and called out to Kelvin, "Oi, come and get it."

With that, he expertly slid down from the roof of the car onto the bonnet, jumped to the ground, leapt over the gate into my yard, grabbed the comic and ran off.

"Thanks!" I shouted sarcastically at the fleeing figure.

I was rewarded with a two-fingered salute as he disappeared around the corner and ran off down the street.

It is that sort of one-off, nothing incident that summed up life at Bluebell Common. Just when you least expected it, when you were most tired, something would happen. Perhaps not serious enough to warrant inclusion in your diary, or calling the police, but enough of an incident to worry you, to trouble you, to cause you to break sweat, to wonder about whether you or your possessions were safe. It was a constant strain, a daily tugging assault on your soul.

Living there meant that you burned more calories emotionally and psychologically than living anywhere else. And if you didn't replenish them, you started to waste away bit by bit until you ran the risk of burning out. Certainly, living there to serve the people meant paying a price, difficult to quantify but always there, like a lead weight you had to carry every day; a burden to take to bed, to the bathroom, whatever you were doing or wherever you went. I could be anywhere doing any job, but I chose to live and work in the most deprived council estate in the metropolitan borough, and there I was paying a little bit of the price each day for making that choice.

So the price I paid that night was to sleep lightly, startled by every bang, every can rattling as it was blown by the wind. Wondering if Kelvin was back, if my car was safe, if someone was climbing on my roof.

The last person to have my job heard rattles, bangs and scrapes as intruders climbed up to the kitchen roof, pulled open an upstairs window, jumped in, walked down the stairs and opened the back door to let the rest of them in. Then the party started: sniffing glue, dropping acid, smoking dope, calling up evil spirits. Making a ouija board seemed such a good idea until it opened the door to something else. Billy called it a piss-taking spirit. Jane called it a clown. Either way it 'told' them what to do next.

That catastrophic night was the culmination of a process which had started with one or two little sins: trespassing in the yard; stealing a bottle of milk from the doorstep; borrowing a quid to get home which would never be paid back. The quid became five, five became a pair of shoes, the shoes became 20 quid and before you knew it, I was told my predecessor was £2,500 down.

£2,500 30 years ago was half my annual stipend. He was supposedly worn down by carrying the weight of living in the lost world of Bluebell Common. I was beginning to get an inkling of the burden that he'd carried. I too was tired that day, but for different reasons; after a weekend away with friends, I was exhausted and looking forward to sleep.

My rest, however, was to be short lived. Two hours after my head hit the pillow, I was awakened by a series of knocks and shouts at my kitchen door. I pulled back my bedroom curtains and looked down. In the weak orange glow of the streetlights, my eyes strained to make out the figure of a woman banging at my door, clearly agitated. I turned the bedroom light on to show them I'd heard and was on my way. Pulling on the first pair of jeans and T-shirt I could find, I made my way downstairs, trying to shake the fog of sleep out of my head.

I opened the door to be greeted by Beth, clearly agitated. She carried a bundle under her arm wrapped in a tea towel. Before I could utter a greeting, she pushed the bundle towards me and I accepted it. This wasn't a conscious action, more of a reflex one. As I picked it up I could hear muffled metallic clanking sounds

"Seth you've got to come quick, Mike has gone mad," she stammered as she cried. "He says he's going to kill us!"

Tears accompanied this information. I was still coming around after being in a deep sleep, and her sobs made it hard for me to make sense of what she was saying. It was obvious she was anxious, upset and fearful, though.

"Beth, come in. Come in," I beckoned.

"No, we've got to get back. Shorty is on his own with him."

Shorty was the affectionate nickname of her four-year-old child from a previous partner. Shorty's dad hadn't stayed around, leaving her during the pregnancy. Mike was the only dad Shorty knew. Beth, Mike and Shorty had entered our fellowship through Baptism preparation classes. After attending church services, they turned up for Bible study. Before long they'd been assimilated into our little congregation at Church House. On the surface they appeared to be a happy little family unit, but scratching the veneer off revealed something worrying. Mike was a veteran. He claimed to have seen action in the Falklands conflict and spoke about being in the Special Forces. He told of missions in Northern Ireland when he'd killed people. This had rung alarm bells with me. I had met Special Forces veterans, I had spoken to men who'd served and seen action. They never spoke about it. Ever. Not to civvies. I didn't buy it. And yet he was certainly troubled.

He claimed to be a martial artist, an expert in Taekwondo. He'd told me he'd used his skills to break an opponent's arms before throwing him from a bridge into a river. Again, this didn't ring true to me. I'd never seen him go to train or heard him talk about the gym he attended. It's been my experience that those who possess an awesome capacity for violence don't feel the need to broadcast it.

As my head began to clear, I started to think in a more logical way. I was holding a bundle, and I hadn't even thought about what it might contain. I set it down on the kitchen work surface, more as a chance for me to gather my thoughts than anything else. I needed to work out what I was going to do next, and in my tired state, my brain could only handle one input at a time. As I pulled back the white linen tea towel, I drew back out of instinct and turned to face Beth. I'd seen was an assortment of knives. Kitchen knives mainly, but one Stanley knife and a large penknife.

In an instant I made the connection. The fog cleared. Beth was frightened because Mike was going to kill the family; she'd bundled up every knife she could find and run to what she thought was a place of safety. She was here because she thought I could help. Suddenly everything else disappeared, and, as I focused on the knives, my heart rate increased and my breathing became fast and shallow. Adrenaline started to pump.

"Beth, we need to call the police," I insisted. "We can't do that. Mike will be taken away. He might go inside, he might be sectioned," she pleaded.

"That doesn't matter at the moment, Beth. Shorty needs to be safe." I underlined my point by gesturing towards the knives.

"No. No police. If you won't help us, I'm going to go back on my own." Beth was adamant.

"Where's Shorty?" I asked, trying to hide my anxiety.

"In bed," she replied, nervously.

"Where was Mike when you left?"

"Downstairs, sat in his chair downstairs," she replied, "Come on."

Why me? *What was I supposed to do*, I thought, but didn't say. Should I involve the police against her wishes? If I did, word would go round the estate that Seth was a grass and it would lead to all kinds of unpleasant consequences. No one would ever trust me again. My work at Bluebell Common would be over.

"I'm going!" Beth insisted.

"I'm coming too." I made a snap decision. Right or wrong? It's easy to judge now, but back then I didn't have the luxury of time to search for the wider ethics of my choice. I was in the moment, when there was only one priority: making sure Shorty and Beth were safe.

As we headed across the green at the centre of our village, the dew soaking my feet, I started to pray that God would be with me, that he would give me the wisdom to say and do what was right. I didn't know what had happened leading up to Mike's threat to kill his family, but I knew I had to help somehow.

"Beth, tell me exactly, and quickly, what's going on."

"I don't know for sure. He hasn't been right all day. No, he hasn't been right for weeks," she corrected herself.

"What do you mean he hasn't been right?"

"It started with him being quiet, which isn't like him. He talks all the time. Telling stories about when he was in the RAF or the SAS. All that stopped. He's been quiet. And then he got picky."

She continued as we drew close to her house. "He's been picking me up on all the little things. Dust on the window ledge, not washing up the moment a plate or a cup has been used. That was bad enough, but then he got angry. Really angry. Shouting over nothing, getting upset over small things. Then tonight, he just turned quiet. He clammed up, didn't say a word. He was sat in his chair looking at me."

"Looking at you, what do you mean?" I asked.

"Staring. He kept staring at me. He didn't say a word for over an hour. He just stared and whenever I left the room he was watching me. And then just before I left he said, 'I'm going to make this family perfect, even if I have to kill every one of us to do it.'"

"Oh Beth, that's awful." We were outside the back door.

"That's when I got all the knives, wrapped them up and came for you," she said.

"So he's just been here on his own for about 10 minutes?" I enquired.

"Yes, if that," she replied.

"This is what I want you to do," I instructed. "I'll go into the lounge and if he's still there, I'll talk to him. You go up to Shorty and make sure he's safe. Don't come in, no matter what you hear. I need to talk with him on his own."

This sounded decisive, as if I had a plan, as if I knew what I was doing. I didn't. I was going to have to wing it. I didn't want Beth to know this, or for her to know how frightened I was. It may not have occurred to Beth, but it did occur to me that Mike might have used his military training already, and he might be preparing to carry his threat out. For all I knew he might have a knife down the side of his chair, ready for him to use to "make his family perfect".

If what he'd told me was true, he could be a formidable foe even without a knife. I suspected that he was a 'Walter Mitty' character in many ways, with his tales of military daring-do and hand-to-hand violence, but I had no way of knowing this for sure. There was still a possibility he was highly trained and could kill with his bare hands. I, on the other hand, had three weeks' training with the Sea Cadets when I was 14, and three years' training with the Church of England. A degree in Philosophy and Theology was no match for an expert with hand-to-hand combat skills.

But here I was anyway, for what it was worth. On my own and facing an unknown threat. I didn't feel brave, or in any way ready. Ironically it was cowardice that was driving me on, the cowardice of worrying about what people would think of me if I didn't help. If I walked away from the situation, everybody would know that Seth Walker had run. That he had no backbone. The inner doubts, the fiery arrows of regret, the poison voice whispering its vile assessment of me would all be proved true.

It's difficult at times to know whether you're acting out of good or bad motives. I've often thought about that and other incidents and wondered whether I did the right thing. I've come to the conclusion that, regardless of my motivation, even if it was because I was worried about what my family or other people would think of me, I was the one who decided to walk into that room, no one else. I didn't know what I'd be facing, or what the outcome would be; I was living in the moment and had made my choice. No matter how badly I thought about myself, I knew that took some measure of resolve. I suppose that regardless of how I felt, or what was driving me forward, I acted in the end out of a sense of good, and hoped some good was to come as a result. Irrespective of whether it was right or wrong at the time, I still faced up to the situation. I ignored my fear and confronted him, despite my misgivings.

I walked in through the back door, turned right and headed into the lounge. It was in darkness. There was some light from the kitchen but it didn't help to quell my fear. The shadows cast by the dim light gave Mike an eerie appearance. The faint glow was reflected in his wide-open eyes. As my eyes adjusted to the dark, I could see that he was staring at me intently, almost as if in hate. As I sat down I could hear Beth's soft footfalls as she went up the stairs to check on Shorty.

Mike continued to stare at me. It was unnerving. I decided to return his gaze, to not break eye contact. My intention wasn't to have a staring competition with him; all I wanted to do was to reflect calmness and strength back at him. I needed to let him see that I wasn't fazed, I wasn't frightened, and more importantly, I wasn't going to be dragged into reacting and matching his hate with my own.

After a while I became aware of my own breathing; it was slowing down, deepening. I was relaxing. This was a good thing. The fear was gone. I was sure I wasn't in the presence of evil but felt sadness more than anything else.

A wave of empathy broke over me. I felt upset for Shorty being brought up with this in the background. I felt sad for Beth who was worried about her daughter and feared that the new life she'd built might come crashing down around her. I also felt sad for Mike. He was a sad man indeed. He was also small. I realised that all the bravado, all the inflated tales of heroism, were because he felt small inside. He had no sense of inner peace or security; he had no good measure of self-esteem left inside him. Life had dealt him a bum hand and now he had no more cards to play. To cope with the day-to-day struggle of life on benefits, of having no job and no hope, he'd projected a big image of himself to the world; yet inside he was empty and felt that he wasn't a proper man.

With this realisation, I felt secure that I could handle the situation, and if it came to it, I could also handle Mike.

His breathing became audibly louder and faster. His eyes widened even more and his face contorted into a snarl. Spittle began to fly out of his mouth as he exhaled.

This was surely going to build to some kind of climax. If I didn't steer the situation, pretty soon it would steer me.

"Mike," I said evenly. "You know that I love you, and I care for you. Don't you?"

It was almost like a balloon being deflated. His breathing changed and the rasping growl began to soften. As I continued to look at him, his eyes began to narrow; the hard edge of anger was dissipating. His head bowed and the rasping sound of harsh breathing changed to sobs as he gave way to his emotions.

I let him cry. I stood up and walked to the door and softly called up to Beth.

"Beth, put the kettle on, it's time we had a nice cup of tea." I needed to communicate to her that it was over, that the threat had passed.

I returned to the lounge, but instead of sitting down I crouched next to Mike and put my arm around him as he continued to sob. We must have been in this position for around five minutes, until we were interrupted by Beth bringing two mugs of tea.

As we sipped at the tea I said, "Mike what's going on?" No great insights, no words of wisdom, just a simple question. He paused and I could see he was thinking. I wondered which Mike we were going to get. Was he going to be honest to us and to himself for perhaps the first time in his adult life, or were we going to hear more fantasy tales of the battlefield?

There was a battle going on alright, but it was inside him. We were at the crux of his issues; if he managed to open up and be honest about who he was and how he felt, then I could point him in the right direction, for counselling, for help, for moving forward. If he made the right choice, that of honesty, then he could start to build himself into the man he was always meant to be.

Mike looked up at me and he spoke. "You know British forces served in Vietnam don't you?" he said. "My dad served in Vietnam and told me all about it." And with that, I knew I'd lost the battle for Mike and that it was a long and rocky road ahead.

"I got the chance to tell my dad I loved him though; he died in my arms. He had a heart attack and I was able to say 'I love you Dad' just as his eyes closed." Mike continued to lay out his Hollywood fantasy.

I listened to many of his tales. Then I offered to pray for him. After the prayer I confronted him.

"Mike, I'm really worried about you. If everything you say is true, you're carrying a burden which is too much for any man to bear." I had to make it appear that I believed all his tales; that I thought he needed help to deal with all he had experienced on the battlefield. I had to deceive him by flattery to get him the help he needed.

"Mike, it's a strong man that asks for help. Please would you see the doctor in the morning?" I pleaded.

I spent no more than a few additional minutes with them. Beth and I were both convinced that Mike posed no immediate problem. However, to be on the safe side, the knives stayed at my house that night. The next morning Mike visited his doctor. A course of counselling was recommended to treat his post-traumatic stress disorder. As a couple they saw it through. As a family they continued to be part of the small church community. I could never be sure that Mike had the capacity to be honest about himself, and therefore I could never feel that I could trust him.

Did some light come out of this dark situation? Perhaps it did. Beth had felt immediate danger; she'd been convinced that the threat to her and her daughter was so great that she removed every knife from the house. Mike had been brought to a crisis point, and even though I felt that he hadn't been able to be honest to me or himself, he had sought help. I often wonder about that little family, whether they stayed the course, whether Mike and Beth are still together. I do know that Beth's faith deepened and it proved a positive influence in her life. She had, at least, found comfort in walking with God.

CHAPTER 9

TWISTED FIRE STARTER

Looking back at my time at Bluebell Common, this is perhaps the most personally disturbing account to write. You see Ron was one of my first converts there. I can't even remember how we first met, but before long he was fully involved in the life of our little, fragile, emerging church family. I had dealt with Ron's close and extended family, so was familiar with the tales that surrounded him, but I was curious to know more. Parts of his narrative jarred and didn't sit comfortably with me. Several months after his conversion to Christianity, I asked him about his life and how he had come to faith. What he told me over the preceding weeks left me with as many questions as answers.

He told me that his family background was not very stable, to say the least. His mum and dad had divorced a few months before he was born, and he said, "You know what that makes me." 50 years ago, when he entered the world, the stigma of being born out of wedlock was real. His mum already had a son who was four years older than him. By the time he was two he had his first spell in care, whilst his mum had another baby, a boy she called Jack.

His father was a vicious man called Dan who lived with them and used to beat his mum and siblings. Chaos called to chaos and the brokenness of that home resulted in broken humans. When he came home from care, his mum had become pregnant again and had a baby girl who she called Sarah Jayne. As the family spiralled down into further destruction, his mum left Dan and the children were put into care. Sarah Jayne and Ron were lucky to be fostered out to a kind family.

I met Ron's mum, Jean, nearly 20 years after these events, which took place at the end of the 1960s. She was a shell of a person, battling her own demons, whilst trying to do her best for the family of young adults who gravitated to her house, directly over the road to me. I tried to paint a smile on my face whenever I visited. The first time I called on her, I let my face show the surprise I felt at the condition of the house, and the look on her face was like a slap to me. I resolved then and there to control myself and be positive. A woman in her situation needed to be built up, and I wanted to help with that.

When he was about four, Ron was taken back home to his mum, who had married a man called Kevin. During this time, he recalls that he was forcibly taken by a man into a shed far away from any help, alone and vulnerable. He remembers that the man wore a chunky gold bracelet and he hurt him in a horrible way. He thought that he could buy his silence with a chocolate bar. Young, isolated, betrayed and violated, Ron felt so dirty, but kept it secret until someone in the family tried to give him the same brand of chocolate. His reluctance led to questions; Mum wondered why he wouldn't eat it, and the story slowly came out. The familiar routine of being collected by the police and returned to a care home followed; he was becoming old before his time.

This time, they were fostered to a family in a different part of town. Sarah Jayne, who was still a toddler, went missing; wanting to explore the world beyond the garden fence, she wandered from safety. Ron recounts that she was found eight hours later in a ditch covered in bite marks. She too had been abused; it should never happen to anyone, let alone a toddler.

The die had been cast and it wasn't long before Ron began his criminal career, at the tender age of six. He thought that he was so slick, but his first clumsy attempt at shoplifting was obvious to the experienced shop-keeper, who'd seen it all before. He was caught and the police were called.

No more cosy foster family homes for Ron; he was placed in a children's home. Two years later, he prayed what was to become a very familiar prayer, for God to get him out of the trouble he was in. If only God would do this, he would follow him forever and never get in trouble again.

In a familiar search for adventure, he'd followed his older sister and her boyfriend as they entered a local church. Whilst they made love up in a balcony, he claimed that he'd played a game of his own, which involved placing lit candles on the altar and knocking one over. It quickly set the altar cloth on fire. Panicking, he ran from the church, his sister and her companion following fast behind. But they'd not gone unnoticed.

The police knocked at the door of the children's home and they were taken into custody. This was becoming old. Frightened and crying tears of hurt, Ron called out to God, "Get me out of this and I'll help you to build a church one day." He wanted to make up for the damage he'd done to God's house. For whatever reason, they never appeared in court, but were cautioned at the police station, with their offence remaining on record. It would be taken into consideration if he got into any trouble again and be added to any punishment that'd be due.

A year later, whilst playing on his own in a secluded wood, he was approached by a group of young men and again assaulted.

Hurt and alone, he made it back to the care home. What he recalled next appalled me then and still does now. He stammered his story out, but the staff wouldn't believe him and washed his mouth out with soap for talking such filth.

"That was what it was like back in the early 1970s" doesn't cut it. I'd like to think we've moved on and that all children are now safeguarded, but harrowing news stories from many towns of young people being betrayed, trafficked, abused and passed round like party favours shows we've a lot of work to do as a society.

As he matured, Ron claimed that some older females took him to bed and introduced him to 'straight sex'.

Three years later something positive at last happened, and he was fostered out to a family, before briefly returning to his mum. She was going through a hard time because her latest husband, Kevin, had hanged himself in the local police cells. When the social worker told him his stepfather had died, he said that he wasn't bothered because he was a mean man who meant nothing to him. He was returned to the foster family, where he felt that he should have been happy, but he couldn't help himself, or more to the point, he did help himself. He'd never had much in the way of money, so he started to steal from the family to try to gain a sense of worth and to give himself options.

It started with a few coins here and there, which he gave to his mum when he saw her. But greed took over and he took their birthday present savings. He was the only suspect and again he found himself taking a ride in a police car to the cells. In trouble again, he repeated the prayer, asking God to get him out of trouble. If he did, then this time Ron would really serve him. This isn't exactly how it played out. 12 months later he was arrested for burglary and sentenced to a stretch in a youth attendance centre.

As time went on, he left school and went to work at the pit on a training scheme. The scheme didn't lead to any employment, so Ron was left with no hope and no future. Aimlessly wandering, he found himself at a fair, talking with the workers.

Soon he was offered a job on the dodgem rides. He burgled several commercial properties, was caught once again and prayed that same prayer again. He was sentenced to a year's probation and an attendance order. He was unemployed once again and drifted for a while before finding himself near a naval base. He saw the ratings in their uniforms, who seemed happy, as if they felt they belonged there. He signed on and started basic training. A fire broke out while he was there and he was considered a suspect. After basic training he was discharged from the Navy back to civilian life.

He headed home, older, with more confidence and slightly wiser. He kept seeing a girl; She'd caught his eye and he couldn't stop thinking about her. He began to feel that this was the person he was going to marry. They started to see each other and within a month they decided to get married. To be sure though, they lived together for a few months first. She already had a daughter, and soon afterwards gave birth to a baby boy. It was around this time that he began to seriously think about God.

They wanted to have the children baptised, and the local church insisted on a baptism preparation course. What was said during the sessions made a lot of sense to Ron and got him thinking about the prayers and promises he'd made to God. He recollected that it was around this time that he first met me, Seth the evangelist from Church House. Something was stirring in his soul; he was getting ready to go to church, but he didn't know which one to attend.

He sought some guidance and bent the knee, praying, "Show me which church to go to." Later that evening, I knocked on his door! Something was happening, he thought, guiding him; the scattered pieces of the jigsaw of his life were beginning to fit together. It seemed a natural progression for him to decide to become a Christian. Ron bowed the knee to Jesus at Church House a few days later and prayed the sinners' prayer with me. We looked at the *Journey into Faith* booklet together. He recited the prayer of commitment and added the following to it: "Show me the way, the truth and the life." This startled me, as I had anticipated that God would want me to share this verse from John chapter 14 verse 6 with Ron: "Jesus said I am the way, the truth and the life, no one comes to the father but through me."

A brutally honest and moving account?

When I first recalled it, I thanked God for the childhood I had experienced, and I'm sure some of you reading this can share those sentiments. Poverty, broken people with no healing on offer, social problems, an underfunded care system struggling to cope, limited state resources and an education system where one size doesn't fit all, contributed to the misery that some at Bluebell Common experienced. 30 years on I'm still working with broken people, products of a broken society. Jesus once said that "The poor you will always have with you." It'd be nice if we could work together to prove him wrong.

Looking back, I remembered that one of my earliest encounters with Ron involved fire. Fire seemed to follow him wherever he went. He mentioned several fires in his story; you may have noticed that he glossed over them, barely mentioning any specific details. In the case of the church fire, he passes it off as an accident, but, as an ex-priest, I know lit candles wouldn't have been left on the altar without a service taking place. Ron may actually believe this , but he may be deluding himself. This inability to be honest, to have a clear understanding of what had made him who he was he was, means he may never be able to fully acknowledge and understand who he came to be.

I remember a fire at Ron's house which he blamed on his mum, Jean. He believes that while drunk, she dropped a lit roll-up down the side of the sofa. She'd been baby-sitting for him and his wife, and when they got home, she was asleep on the sofa. They roused her, thanked her and sent her on her way, before heading up to bed. While the family slept, Ron recalled, the cigarette smoldered and set the sofa alight; it spewed poisonous fumes and the family were lucky to escape with their lives.

At this point I was not aware that Ron had been associated with several fires. Could it be that his personality was so broken that he found expression through flames? I'd first met him and his wife through baptism preparation sessions. I was aware that he was eager to belong and was looking for some deeper meaning to his life, and I thought that he had a lot to offer.

Ron and his family were moved from the fire-damaged house to a vacant property just 10 houses from me. I went to see them there to see how they were and whether there was anything I could do to help. He seemed agitated. I asked him what was wrong, and he took me outside to tell me how the fire had led to yet more serious problems for him.

Ron's neighbour at the fire-damaged property was a young mother who was living on her own, caring for her two children. She wasn't a single parent in the traditional sense; she was committed to her husband, Mitch, but he was away from home. His children believed he was working on the oil rigs, but he was allegedly coming to the end of a seven-year stretch for being part of a group of active armed robbers.

Mitch had heard about the house fire and blamed it on Ron. Perhaps he knew far more about Ron and his unfortunate associations with fire than I did. Mitch felt that he'd endangered his wife and children and now he wanted to make Ron pay for it. Ron was told that when he got out, Mitch would tap dance on his ribs. He was desperate; I could see he was frightened of Mitch and knew what he was capable of. He begged me to help him.

I was puzzled and couldn't make sense of it. Why would this Mitch be so angry? It was a house fire, an accident. It didn't add up to me.

Despite my misgivings I agreed to go and visit Mitch's wife and plead for mercy. This didn't prove to be straightforward; she was adamant that Ron was to blame. However, I appealed on behalf of the family, removing Ron from the equation and focusing on how traumatic a dad's beating would be for his children. After a while, with gentle persistence on my part, she reluctantly agreed to call Mitch off.

Occasionally, very occasionally, my family would visit me at Bluebell Common. Not my parents, but my sister visited and my younger brother stayed over once.

I think it was significant for him because he still speaks about it to this day. He is not a naive person. 30 years ago he was a bricklayer by day and a bouncer at night. He's seen his fair share of what life has to offer.

He is a Liverpool Football Club fan. The date was May 14th 1988 – FA Cup Final day. Liverpool were playing Wimbledon, a match of football brain versus brawn. There was no way he'd miss this match. Prior to arranging the visit, I had agreed to watch the Final at Ron's house. I explained to my brother to be on his guard and not to react if it was different to what he was used to.

We turned up with some brews; after all, beer and football go together.

As we entered Ron's house my brother greeted him, held up his four pack and asked where the fridge was. "We haven't got one," was the reply. "Go and put them in the bath."

He later told me that tubs of margarine, bottles of milk and cans of beer were floating in a few inches of cool water in the bath. On that day he got a fresh appreciation of the life I was observing and living.

I have so much more to tell concerning Ron and his obsession with fire but I have decided to keep my silence. Out of all the people I dealt with during my ministry, he's the one who troubles me most. The lack of certainty that he'd recovered from the damage of the past, that the inferno that followed him around had been put out, means I can't let my guard down. I don't mind admitting that I worry one day he'll knock on my door and the past will come to call.

Chapter 10

IT'S THE DEVIL'S NIGHT TONIGHT

Dennis was the closest person in appearance to Father Christmas I've ever come across. The only difference is he wasn't grey; his hair and beard were brown, seasoned with a small pinch of grey. His eyes seemed to have a constant twinkle, complemented by rosy cheeks. A smile wasn't usually far from his lips.

He radiated love and was quick to show his emotions. I've seen his face convulsed with laughter, creased with concern and bathed in tears. However, I'd never seen him angry.

As a young man he was a soldier and served part of his national service in Borneo, in what is now the Malaysian state of Sarawak. The army spent time tracking and fighting communist rebels in the harsh environment of dense tropical rainforest. But what changed Dennis's life there didn't involve patrols or fire fights: it was dealing with those who gave their life during military action. He, along with his fellow soldiers, had the task of placing corpses into body bags. Working with those who'd died, sometimes in horrendous ways, was to have a profound and long-term impact on him. It changed his life, and not for the better.

While in Borneo he didn't have the time to think about or deal with his experiences; he just lived through them. With demobilisation came the chance to adjust to civilian life. However, he couldn't make sense or sufficiently process the sights he'd seen or the things he'd experienced whilst on active duty. Instead of dealing with the terror and sadness, he pushed them down, deep down, and sought release in other ways. Unfortunately he couldn't suppress them forever and they started to find expression through a growing sense of anger.

He turned to the physical disciplines of power-lifting and karate to channel the anger that had started to consume him.

No talking therapy was on offer in the late 1960s, and he had to find his own way of dealing with his pain.

In time-honoured fashion, he followed the dictates of contemporary society and tried to settle down. He had married his long-term girlfriend, but this had failed to help him to adjust to life as a civilian. He began to drink, not the controlled recreational drinking that many people enjoy, but drinking to forget. Not for him two or three pints and friendly banter in a club or bar: he drank to excess. And when he was sufficiently drunk, he would return home.

Under the influence of post-traumatic stress disorder, alcohol and a wealth of regrets, his anger found an outlet in physical violence, which was unfortunately directed at his wife, he told me. During the years that she stood by him, he repaid her loyalty with beating after beating. After one severe attack, her cheekbone had to be surgically reconstructed.

When he was at his lowest, consumed with self-loathing, he stumbled into church and had an experience that would change his life forever. Dennis was completely broken down by that experience; he said he felt God's love fill every corner of his being. He described a light shining into the darkest chambers of his heart. A door was flung wide open and he felt that he'd been released from a dark, dank dungeon. A transformation was taking place and he felt more alive than ever.

That is when love started to replace the hate in his life. Anger was banished and, in its place, in swept empathy. He had a newfound gift of empathic intuition which would see him shed tears as he experienced the sadness of those he ministered to. He not only shared, but experienced people's pain and sadness and was able to help to guide them to a place of acceptance, love and even happiness.

His wife was relieved at first. They were reconciled and their marriage was salvaged from the wreckage of many years of violence. However, she could never fully believe that this was a new Dennis who had re-entered her life, and could you blame her? So when her doubts began to grow, she would chide him to see if he would react. When he only responded with love, she'd still have her doubts, and the chiding would lead to name calling and occasionally even physical violence. She just had to know that he had changed, that he would never raise his fist to her again. If he didn't rise to the bait, she would finally be sure that she'd be safe. Sadly this never happened, and she always worried that the peace would one day be shattered. For all the time I knew him, however, Dennis never once returned to his old ways.

One of the gifts that he felt God had given him in place of the anger that had previously driven him, was an intuitive sensitivity.

He described it as hearing God's voice. He would have a conviction that he should go somewhere, perhaps to visit someone who was in difficulty, or maybe to take some food to the homeless under the bridge. Twice he believed that this voice had proved to be right beyond any doubt, and both occasions led to dramatic conclusions.

The first of these began whilst he was in the bath at home. He felt that God was telling him to get up, get dressed and go to town. He went to the kitchen and started to make some marmalade sandwiches. He thought God was urging him to go and visit the homeless people under the south bridge, as he regularly did, to take them some food and give them some company. But as he started to spread the butter, he felt a strong conviction that he should leave immediately and head to town.

When he got off the bus, he didn't know where to go, so he just walked in any direction and found himself at the doors of the parish church in the town centre. It is an impressive Victorian building, with the largest tower in the district. Over the years the wear and tear of urban life has taken its toll and it's been undergoing much-needed restoration and building work.

As he approached the stone structure, he looked up and noticed an orange glow. At first he thought a service must be taking place and the church was lit up from within. But no hymns were being sung, no prayers were being said. He tried to turn the door handle but it wouldn't open. He then caught the acrid smell of smoke. He realised that the orange glow was in fact the light from dancing flames; the church was on fire.

He rushed to a phone box (remember those?) and dialed 999. The Fire Brigade worked hard and managed to save the structure of the building and limit the damage to its internal fixtures and furniture. Faulty wiring in the newly installed under-pew heating had caused the blaze. The damage took several months to repair and a commemoration was planned for its completion, to which Dennis was invited.

IT'S THE DEVIL'S NIGHT TONIGHT

The second occasion was very significant to my predecessor, and to the young people who had taken over his life. One evening while at home, Dennis was suddenly convinced that he had to get up, leave the house and head for Bluebell Common. He had no idea where exactly he was going or what he was to do when he got there; he only knew that he had to go. A strong compulsion was pushing him away from his home and pulling him towards Bluebell Common. He was sure God was telling him to: that was reason enough.

Dennis had no car, and the two-mile journey took him nearly 40 minutes on foot. There's a dual carriageway at the bottom of the village, with one road leading in and out. Bluebell Common was designed in a crude figure of eight, with houses built on either side of the streets, and horizontally bisected by a road two thirds of the way up. As you stand at the bottom of the village, you see the war memorial in front of you, its faded wreaths and brass memorial plaques telling their story of loss and sacrifice. If you turn left and walk on, the road curves round and straightens, running up for nearly half a mile, until turning again at the top, where its name changes from North Street to Spinney Road. Here it runs parallel to an old straight track, known as the Wicken Way. It's believed to be the remains of a Roman road, with local historians finding sufficient artifacts to be sure of this. The road then runs half a mile down a gentle hill, eventually curving back to the war memorial and the one road in and out of the estate.

That night Dennis was facing the wall memorial and had to decide whether to walk left or right. He felt compelled to turn left and, once again, he obeyed that inner conviction. As he began to walk up North Street, he felt drawn to cross the road so that he was walking on the side where Church House was situated. All the while he kept asking God, "Where should I go?" As he drew nearer, he knew Church House was to be his destination. Although the hour was late, lights were on as he walked through the gate and rapped loudly on the living room window.

A knock on a door or window is an everyday, mundane action, so why was this knock so significant? Because at the very moment Dennis was banging loudly at the window, Jane was, in her words, "sparking up my lighter". My predecessor was sat tied to a chair with a lighter fluid-soaked blanket over his head, with the young people, as I have been told on several occasions, about to set him on fire.

I have subsequently discussed that night with Jane. As she talked to me, her two-year-old son played at her feet. She told me he was conceived in the bed upstairs in Church House and was the child of one of the young people who was present on that fateful night. Jane said they had been sniffing glue and dropping acid when someone had decided they should try a ouija board. She claims that they had called up a 'piss-taking' spirit which told them to murder my predecessor.

Her story tallied with what I'd previously heard from another source. She says that when the knocking at the window happened, it was as if a spell had been broken. Almost as if coming out of a hypnotic trance, the young people came to and looked at each other in disbelief, not comprehending what had happened. They couldn't explain how the situation had developed to this disturbing and potentially tragic point. Whether you believe that Dennis was acting under the direction of a higher power, or the whole thing was just a coincidence, the result was the same. He arrived at just the right time. He not only probably saved my predecessor's life, but also in another sense saved the young people's lives. It's hard enough surviving as part of an underclass: unemployed, with no qualifications, living in a sink estate as the acceptable casualties of a broken economic system. It would have been nigh on impossible for them to have made anything of their lives with a murder conviction on their records.

When I arrived, and started working at Bluebell Common, Dennis was one of the first people who stepped forward to offer me some support. He said he thought it was important that he got involved and that he'd back me up no matter what. It was an offer I welcomed, but I wasn't then aware of how significant his companionship and generous use of his gifts was to prove.

Without the context of knowing Dennis, I am aware his story stretches the bounds of credibility. Despite this, for me, living in that situation, facing these problems on a daily basis, I was glad that Dennis was there, with his quiet strength, gifts of sensitivity and intuition, and his willingness to follow his inner voice.

It was a dark, late autumnal night. Dennis and I were stood in an alleyway praying. It may sound unusual, but we used to do this under the cover of darkness, taking the church onto the streets. This alleyway runs half the length of North Street and forms the boundary between the front of the houses and a central green. When the estate was built, the houses were constructed so that the rear door of each property was in the kitchen and faced the street. The front of the properties faced the central green area. It was a concept designed to engender a sense of community, with a focal point that spoke of leisure and green spaces, in contrast to the dusty darkness of the pit that the men spent their days toiling in.

The central green area was mainly made up of playing fields, but there were also two buildings which were at the heart of the life of the community. One was a nursery and infant school, the other a miners' welfare club.

It takes some doing, explaining why the houses were built back to front, but it worked. You have to visit to get a flavour of what the planners had in mind. On a summer evening people talk over the back gate, or sit in the yard, tinkering with cars, nattering and sharing a drink.

On that night Dennis and I were on a prayer walk. It's something that we did on a regular basis, at night when curtains were drawn and doors were tightly shut. We would wander through the village praying for the residents, unaware this act of care was taking place.

At certain points Dennis would stop me and pray, as if he had an insight. Sometimes he would tell me I should visit a particular house. Him saying, "I'm getting a sense of sadness here," would prompt a visit and some much-needed ministry. Invariably he'd be right. I would call round the next day, explaining it was just a routine visit, and would often hear a tale of woe. As a skeptic I often wonder whether this was evidence of a God-given gift, or whether everyone on the estate felt sad at some point. We all have some sadness in our lives: a still-harboured grief; regret for a bad decision made or a good choice that we failed to make, chipping away at our emotional wellbeing. Was it a self-fulfilling prophecy to go round and steer the conversation to any sense of sadness that the resident might have been feeling? Some would say yes. Perhaps that's true, but it did give my parishioners the chance to talk, to share, to get their regrets and sadness out in the open.

However, on that night, we were to do something different, something that even today fills me with a sense of dread and fear when I think about it. I am a fell runner; I run mainly on my own and for five months of the year I may run at night. Like many runners I use a head torch; its narrow but bright beam provides a corridor of light in the gloom of a country night. Sometimes the moon is so bright that I don't even switch the torch on; other times mist reduces visibility to a few feet as white spectral clouds glide past. I may be two miles from the nearest house; the night has many voices: the call of rutting deer, the bark of a fox, the owl's mournful cry, and yet I've never since felt the fear of the dark that I was to experience with Dennis that night.

As we prayed in this alleyway, Dennis nudged me and said, "The devil's night tonight. Does that mean anything to you?"

Again the skeptics among us may see this as a medium's typical tactic, firing out many different pieces of information and asking a single client or an assembled crowd to make sense of them. Invariably, people will then try to make what is being said fit in with their life.

However, on this occasion, I didn't have to try hard to find a match. A quarter of a mile from where we were standing along the old straight track was a small, isolated area of housing. I had heard, and I can't remember who from, of tales of satanic worship taking place there. This immediately popped into my mind in response to Dennis's unusual question.

I told him about these rumours and he said, "Let's take a little walk, Seth, and see what we can find."

Dennis had a confidence that I didn't feel. I was unnerved and felt increasingly uneasy. I couldn't explain it, but I felt weak; I didn't feel safe at all. There were just two of us walking to I didn't exactly know where, to face I didn't exactly know what. We could've been heading towards a larger gathering of people in league with our spiritual enemy. Or not. Tittle tattle, a dark, windy night and the prospect of a walk on an unlit track may have been a more plausible explanation for my anxiety. Whatever the reason, I was in the grip of real fear and growing dread.

Dennis took us up to the top of North Street, and we walked through a small alleyway onto the old straight track. Turning left, we headed south, walking for 200 metres, relying on the moonlight to avoid puddles and the embedded stones which could trip us up. We emerged from the ridge where it crossed a road and turned right.

We could see five houses grouped together at the side of the road. As we drew closer, we noticed a number of cars parked on the side of the road and on the driveway of one house in particular. Dennis felt this was significant and we walked past, praying. He prayed that God's light would shine into that house and drive away any darkness. We walked on for five minutes in the dark. I didn't know why; perhaps Dennis was obeying one of his inner voices.

We were still praying when Dennis stiffened and hesitated. Regaining composure he concluded his prayer, then turned to head back towards Bluebell Common. As we approached the houses again, we noticed that something was different. There were no cars parked on the road and only one car remained on the driveway. Dennis turned to me and said, "Do you think we might have broken that party up?"

I didn't know what to say. We walked on and soon came to the track where we turned left and walked away from the orange glow of the streetlights. As we stopped to let our eyes adjust to the darkness, I got the unnerving sensation we were not alone. I felt that we were being watched, and I was again struck with a growing sense of dread. I felt a sensitivity at the top of my neck and now knew what spine-tingling fear was. Dennis lifted his head, turned it to one side and said, "Come on lad."

We walked along the old straight track in silence, ears straining to hear the scrape of a following footstep. It took all my resolve not to speed up and break into a run. When we reached the alleyway leading to North Street, I felt a huge sense of relief. The fear had dissipated as quickly as it had arrived. The only way I can describe it is like when you walk into a shop on a cold day and they have a heater blowing down from on top of the doorway. A warm sense of peace replaced the cold fear. Dennis stopped us, turned around and looked towards the alleyway.

"I think we've been followed," he said.

I knew what he meant, but whatever or whoever it was had remained in the shadows of the old straight track, and I never walked it in darkness again.

IT'S THE DEVIL'S NIGHT TONIGHT

A week later, Dennis and I were praying in my study. He was concerned that the house had not been cleansed after the incident with the ouija board several years before. He thought that a mocking spirit was directing its energy towards me.

Meanwhile a lady had started to help us in our work; she would attend our Bible studies alongside her husband, and counsel people who were facing problems. At one point she had become agitated during prayers and told me that the image of a clown's head had popped into her head, stopping her praying.

This could all have been a set of coincidences, or an attempt by those involved to somehow make sense of what had happened in Church House. Had Dennis made a mistake in thinking he had detecting the presence of a mocking spirit? Did the lady already know what the young people had done? That might explain her thinking of a clown during prayer.

Whatever the truth, Dennis had been concerned enough to ask to come and pray with me in my study. We were meditating in silence on the nature of God's love, with a lit candle and a crucifix resting on the desk that I composed my sermons on.

Dennis broke the silence: "We hate Seth Walker," he whispered in an even tone. "We can't get him because his faith is too strong, but he can trip himself up."

I asked him why he'd said those words.

"I don't know why," he replied. "It just came into my head."

I recalled this bizarre message later, when I found myself alone, away from any help, with a man who said he was being told to kill me.

I spoke with my boss, James, the minister, about what Dennis had felt in the house. I asked whether the house had been blessed prior to my arrival.

It had not, so an appointment was made and the minister arrived. We went from room to room praying, the minister holding a tabletop crucifix before him which he'd fetched from the chapel, as he blessed each room in turn. The last room was my bedroom. As we left, I noticed the smell of animal faeces; I looked into the small guest bedroom, and there in the centre of the carpet was a pile of dog excrement. My pet dog had opened its bowels in this room: an unfortunate occurrence I, like many other dog owners, had witnessed before. I hastily cleaned it up and sprayed air freshener. The minister seemed to believe this to be a metaphor for the dark, demonic, filthy influences leaving the house.

When he'd left, and I had tidied away the cups and biscuits plate, I reached for the crucifix to take back to the chapel. As I picked it up something didn't seem quite right. It wasn't immediately obvious, but I couldn't shake that feeling off.

Looking from the top to the bottom of the crucifix I noticed that it included a small sign, a replica of the notice supposedly placed on Jesus's crucifix in mockery by Pontius Pilate: "INRI", standing for "Jesus the Nazarene, King of the Jews". It was attached to the cross by a single rivet; that rivet had worked loose, and the sign had been inverted. Whether the sign had been upside down during the whole of the blessing or it'd only just happened, I didn't know. I did, however, feel that it had made a mockery of the blessing. A process that should have brought me comfort and reassurance had left me feeling deeply troubled instead.

I felt that I was no further forward, and a sense of unease continued to plague me. Dennis said that he thought whatever was in the house was still there and was playing games with me. As a skeptic, looking back, I can see how all this talk was bound to lead to anxiety. It's no surprise I found it difficult to find peace in my own home.

Several months later, I hosted the quarterly gathering of my fellow urban evangelists: Five of us, who worked for the church nationwide, carrying out this challenging role. We worked in some of the most deprived areas of the country, often feeling isolated and sometimes misunderstood. One of my colleagues was sufficiently concerned about how the house made him feel that he offered to come back with two of his colleagues to pray. I took them up on the offer, and his boss, an author who had a successful, charismatic evangelical ministry, led the prayers. As we went from room to room, they seemed to be restoring a more peaceful atmosphere.

We remained in the study for the longest time. As we sat down over tea and biscuits, after the house blessing, the spectre of a clown was again raised. Whether I had previously spoken to my colleague about it, and he had related it to his boss, or whether it was somehow communicated supernaturally to him, I don't know, but he was convinced that a presence identifying as a clown had been infesting the property. He was confident that the prayers had done their job and I would have no further trouble. I am not sure whether this was the result of authentic spiritual warfare, or the reassuring bearing of this tall, confident man of God, but I never felt troubled in the house again.

During my time in the village, Dennis started to lose contact with the church. Something was happening in his life; he had discovered an outlet for his unexpressed feelings: a creative writing class, which was no small task for him. Initially Dennis wasn't completely literate; his writing needed revision as he learned the rules of grammar and syntax. However, his writing had power; it conveyed emotions and truth and convinced those who read it.

Over the course of a year he developed as a writer, and saw some of his prose published locally. On one of my last encounters with him, he told me had been invited to live within a creative community. He took this opportunity, and that was the last I ever saw or heard of him.

You can explain away every one of these incidents involving Dennis as coincidences, or self-fulfilling prophecies. However, I am convinced that there was something genuine at the heart of his gift. He acted out of deep love, with empathy and sincerity, leading invariably to something good.

I suppose that as you look at Dennis's life, and see how love replaced anger, and hope replaced despair, you can't fail to reach the conclusion that it is possible to change, to be born again.

Chapter 11

UNLEADED POSTCARD

Phase three of the improvement scheme to bring Bluebell Common accommodation into the 1980s was in full swing. It was running the risk of going over budget because of the amount of overnight theft from properties being refurbished. A margin for 'shrinkage' is always built in to schemes like this, but it had already been exceeded several weeks previously. When the foremen, contractors and sub-contractors left the site at night, certain members of the community would move into the properties, looking for something to use or sell.

I saw new doors being carried away for use as kindling; I heard of radiators being removed and new gas boilers being uninstalled and sold to local plumbers. It wasn't uncommon to see double-glazed window units being removed from houses on the same evening they'd been installed.

The powers-that-be thought better to employ a local person, who may themselves have form, as a security guard to bring a halt to the thefts. Unfortunately for me, their choice was always going to lead to trouble. Whether by design or by accident, they decided to set a thief to catch a thief: Shortland, the supposed ex-Hells Angel who had beaten Barry, seduced his wife and driven him from his home.

The project had brought some benefits with it beyond improved living condition: residents were also being employed. One of our most active parishioner's sons was working on the redevelopment as a labourer. He began to tell his mother that Shortland was telling all who'd listen that he'd caught me climbing out of one of the properties in his charge with a bag of cement over my shoulder. He claimed he'd threatened to report me and call the police, but had let me go out of the goodness of his heart.

The fact that this alleged encounter had taken place while I was leading a parish Bible study shows how laughable the whole thing was: just another tale for me to shrug off and chalk up to experience. As my boss once said to me of his parishioners, "What they don't know about you, they make up."

However, Shortland persisted in telling this story, insisting it was true despite people's doubts. When the tale began to grow in the telling, and I was supposedly caught carrying out tools as well, I decided enough was enough.

I called in to the site office, a Portakabin with wire mesh-covered windows, and asked to speak to the site manager. He was easy to spot, the only one wearing a tie.

I explained who I was and about my role within the village. I also asked him if he was aware of any incidents which had been reported concerning me.

He said he hadn't heard anything, although he was curious why I was asking. Perhaps I should've brushed it off and not taken it any further. I'd thought long and hard about what action to take and knew there'd be repercussions. However, I not only had my reputation to think of, but that of the church. This kind of scandal could put our work in jeopardy if I allowed these unfounded rumours to continue.

I explained about Shortland, and told the site manager it wasn't a one-off, but that he'd persisted in repeating these allegations.

Not only did I receive a verbal apology, but also an assurance that the matter would be dealt with. The site manager scribbled a note for me on headed paper, officially recording the apology. I left feeling satisfied I'd done what was needed to be done, but I suspected there was more to come.

I didn't know how Shortland's employers already felt about him; there were clearly other issues which they took into consideration, and he was dismissed within the hour.

I became aware of this shortly afterwards, because he didn't go quietly, launching into a tirade in which he threatened to make me pay.

Jim, the parishioner's labourer son, told me about this. He was a tough man; in his earlier years he'd been a skilled amateur boxer and was a well-known street fighter. I once had to go to a local pub to retrieve his football kit which he'd left there after a fight – when I say a fight, it wasn't the sort of one-on-one street fight that I normally witnessed at Bluebell Common, but more a wild west saloon brawl. After a Saturday league football game, Jim and his brother were having a few pints and relaxing in the pub, as were several members of a local rugby team, who were celebrating a win. Whether the rugby boys were a little too exuberant for the brother's liking, or whether the brothers upset the rugby players, I don't know, but a fight ensued. Jim said he was holding his own and decking one rugby player after another, when he looked over to see how his brother was doing. While he was distracted, someone grabbed a handful of Jim's hair and smashed his head down onto the side of the pool table. That was the last he remembered for a while.

They never prepare you for situations like that in theological college, but I found myself later that evening talking to the pub landlord, and bringing back the brothers' football kits.

My willingness to enter hostile territory to return his belongings seemed to win me some kudos in his eyes: a debt that he was paying back now, with a warning. To watch Shortland, because he was sly and capable of anything.

I spoke earlier about the overheads of living in Bluebell Common. the added emotional calories to be burnt just by living there. Here was a case in point. A man who I'd been told had a history of violence, who would stop at nothing, had threatened to pay me back. My shoulders sagged with the unseen weight of the threat.

A sense of dread sat in the background of everyday life, an emotional drain adding effort to everything I did. Making a cup of tea wasn't just a routine task, it was making a cup of tea whilst being worried for my safety. I wasn't terrified, but I was certainly afraid. The vague nature of the threat made it even more insidious; how would he pay me back? What did he mean by "get me"? When would it happen? Would he leave it on the back burner, to serve up in good measure when I least expected it?

The strain had started to take its toll on me. During the night I would start at every sound, wondering whether this was Shortland coming to make good on his word. The relief of sleep became harder to achieve and this fed my anxiety.

I wasn't reassured when I was warned to tape up my letterbox at night because he was going to give me an 'unleaded postcard': a quantity of petrol poured through the letterbox and then lit. I had to take this threat seriously.

I went out to a hardware store and bought a pickaxe handle and a roll of strong duct tape. I put the pickaxe handle under my bed, within easy reach. And each night I'd tape my letterbox shut from the inside. I applied layer upon layer of tape until the letterbox was secured and couldn't be budged.

Around this time I fell ill; doubtless I was run down and susceptible to infection. There'd been a flu epidemic and I took to my bed. It took two weeks to get back to anywhere near good health. At the height of the fever I'd neither the time nor the energy to block my letterbox, or even to worry. It took all of my resources to cope with being so ill.

As I recovered, I suddenly realised that I was no longer afraid. And I never did tape my letterbox up again. I had worked out that Shortland's greatest weapon wasn't actual violence, but the threat of it. Throughout my time at Bluebell Common, it had been my experience that 90 per cent of threats were never acted upon. If someone means you harm, they are going to harm you then and there, when their blood is up and their anger takes away reason, not at a later date when they've calmed down and reason can prevail.

Charged with fresh vigour as the strength returned to my limbs, I threw myself into daily workouts at the youth club. The discipline of lifting weights, running and playing team sports was the tonic I had needed, and my mood lifted.

One day, as I was returning home, walking down the alleyway between the front of the houses on North Street and the green, I noticed a familiar figure approaching me. It wasn't just familiar, but well known to me. It was Shortland. I'd know his weasel-like face anywhere. It had caused me weeks, months of anguish, and there he was. I don't know if he was expecting me to turn and run, or to cross the green, or to speed down one of the driveways, but I didn't. I'd worked out that nothing was going to happen, and even if it did, It'd be over far quicker than the weeks and months I had spent worrying about its arrival.

As we got within 30 yards, he looked up and noticed me for the first time. His eyes narrowed as he fixed them on me. I met his gaze and smiled. I didn't falter but kept walking. 20 yards now and closing; in just a few seconds we'd meet. I took my hands out of my pockets where they'd been keeping warm, balled each hand into a fist, but kept on swinging them by my sides as I walked. I didn't want to look threatening, but I wasn't going to slouch like a victim either. The way you carry yourself on the street is one of the first steps of self-defence. A bully is after an easy victim, not someone who's walking with confidence, who's aware of his surroundings and isn't showing fear.

10 yards: I'm still smiling, he's not. I raise my right fist, intending to extend my hand for him to shake, to see how he will react. We continue to close on each other.

Five yards: he turns and walks down an access way. I walk on.

After a few seconds, I looked over my shoulder in case he'd doubled back, but he hadn't. I'd faced my fear. In the words of ancient oriental folklore, I'd smeared charcoal on the face of the ghost. He wouldn't haunt me again.

No more threats were ever relayed to me from Shortland. Although it was a difficult time for me, I also learned lessons and grew. That incident has taught me that fear is the biggest drainer of confidence, and, more importantly, facing your fear is far better than cowering from it.

Chapter 12

WRESTLING WITH DAVE

We were walking across the green towards the lake which runs along the north side of Bluebell Common – we being Tristan and me. Tristan was visiting from a leafy suburban southern town popular with city commuters. He attended the affluent church that contributed half my stipend and wanted to see what life was like in the lost world of Bluebell Common; a kind of council estate safari with me as the guide, the tracker who'll follow the spoor and show him life in the raw. Tourism with a twist. He'd travelled up north with that in mind, like an olden-day missionary. He'd journeyed to a jungle; not a jungle of succulent plants and trees, but a redbrick jungle made up of broken lives, intertwined just like the vines growing through fallen tree trunks on a real rainforest floor.

Tristan wasn't wearing khaki fatigues or a pith helmet like missionaries of old. He was resplendent in Barbour jacket, Pringle jumper and tailored slacks.

The green separates Larkwood, the mother parish, from Bluebell Common, the mission village. We'd been visiting the big church up on Larkwood estate, originally built as a model pit village to house the miners of Bradley colliery and their families. At the heart of the village was a parish church, a doctors' surgery and a junior and infant school. Perhaps heart of the village is the wrong phrase to use – I'd been told that the heart of the village had been ripped out when they closed the pit and pulled down the headgear not long after the miners' strike of '84; unemployment was now rife. An elderly retired miner told me that they'd left a rich seam of coal underground stretching all the way to Brinsley, five miles distant, and in the process had entombed millions of pounds worth of machinery. That wasn't all that got buried. Hopes, dreams and an income stream for a community were sealed below ground when they capped the main shaft. Now there was nothing for fathers, sons and brothers to do. The male population went from breadwinner to dependent overnight. Pride was lost, a community was neutered and little was gained.

The green was part of the recreation facilities provided for the miners a century ago when the pits were booming. As we walked down the gently sloping hill, past large beech trees, I noticed a figure hitting a golf ball enthusiastically with a metal club.

Dave was the last person in the world I needed to see at that moment, let alone with a golf club in his hand. He was part of a large extended family who took up about two thirds of my time. Just two weeks ago we'd been rolling around his living room floor fighting, and now here he was in front of me swinging a golf club.

It'd been a Thursday night; an evangelist was performing at the big parish church and I was required to be there. However, I couldn't summon up the enthusiasm to go and see this man preach; he was a friend of the rector and I'd heard him preach on several occasions, but I was not a fan. With that in mind I was slow to prepare, late to set off and late to arrive.

I walked up past the graveyard, making my way round to the church entrance to be greeted by Dave in a state of extreme agitation, with one of the churchwardens frantically trying to calm him down.

"Let me in. I want to go inside the church."

Dave was clearly under the influence of alcohol. He was also very angry and agitated, pacing backwards and forwards clenching and unclenching his balled fists. He turned around towards the church door and took two steps towards the opening. Brian the churchwarden stood firm, blocking his way. Brian had worked down the pit for 30 years and was no push over.

"Now then, you can't come in here carrying on like that, lad!"

"Hello Brian, is everything alright?" I asked over Dave's shoulder.

"This here fella is drunk. He's been carrying on, shouting and swearing, and kicking the chairs around at the back of the church. We can't have him in, Seth."

"Hello Dave, what's to do here then?" I asked, but he didn't reply. He was clearly drunk and his clenched fists hinted at his emotional state.

"Oh he's one of yours is he, Seth?" Brian interrupted.

One of mine, one of mine. I didn't like the implications of that phrase. But there was no time for discussion. Dave was obviously angry, drunk and, no doubt, had a story to tell. In telling it, he might vent enough anger to diffuse the situation, but this wasn't the place to do it.

"I know him, Brian", I said. "I'll have a word with him and maybe I'll be able to calm him down."

Regularly dealing with drunk people helps you to develop a skill set, a checklist if you will, which you can use to work out what your next action should be. Dave wasn't presenting as a happy drunk, a friendly drunk, someone to share a song or a joke with before parting happily. He wasn't a maudlin drunk bemoaning his poor lot. He was an angry drunk: in my growing experience the worst kind to deal with. When people are angry, generally reason doesn't win out. Even if they know they're wrong, the anger pushes them to act in a way that runs counter to all the best evidence. How many of us have continued to rage in the grip of an argument with a loved one, despite knowing full well we're in the wrong and they're in the right? Add eight pints of bitter to this anger, and reasoning is about as effective as bringing a carrot to a knife fight.

"Now then Dave, they're not going to let us in," I said, to indicate we were in this together.

"Why don't you come with me and we'll have a wander and a natter," I suggested. I stood between Dave and the church, with my open hands, not fists, held up at shoulder height, almost like a surrender gesture. I wanted to defuse the situation, to show I was no threat, to let Dave de-escalate and regulate his fury.

"No! I want to come in. I need to be in the church." He jabbed at my chest with his finger to emphasise his point.

"Why do you need to be in the church, Dave?" I enquired, lowering my hands.

"I just do. I've just buried my gran and I've had a skin-full and I want to talk to God."

I was trying to remove Dave from the situation. To put as many miles between him and the church as possible. To let him begin to sober up and then help him, whatever that looked like. I could've driven him miles from the church if I'd had my car with me. But I didn't: it'd broken down and was being fixed by one of the estate's self-taught backyard mechanics. How then was I going to shift him and stop him from going back inside the church and rage against God?

"Well, you won't get a chance to talk to God in there will you?" I asked. "What with all the guitars and tambourines and singing. Why don't you come for a walk with me along the old straight track and talk about it and we'll see what we can do."

He paused, swayed a little and his eyes narrowed to slits. *Here we go*, I thought, resigned to a struggle. But it was not to be; he softened.

"Come on then."

As we walked, a diatribe of anger followed, directed at God and me as his representative, because Dave's grandma had died unjustly. It didn't matter that she was in her late 60s, not a bad innings considering the widespread poverty in the area. It didn't matter that she was a lifelong smoker and had died of lung cancer. It just wasn't right. Why had God so cruelly plucked his gran from him? It was pathetic; Dave was reverting to type and doing what he always did, playing the victim. Poor me, poor me, pour me another drink.

We had been walking for about half an hour when I realised we were heading back towards the church. This might pose a problem, but Dave's house was on the way there. I had an idea: why not suggest we stop and have a cup of tea? By then the service would be over and we could go back into the church without disturbing anything.

"Now then Dave, how about we pop in, put the kettle on and have a cuppa? I don't know about you but I'm spitting feathers."

"Aye, good idea. And I can have a slash, I'm busting," he replied.

We entered the house and while he disappeared upstairs, I headed for the front room. Dave's wife Janine was asleep on the sofa. I felt uncomfortable, like I was intruding. I backed up, turning towards the kitchen. I lifted the kettle towards the sink, filled it, set it back down and switched it on. I started to search for teabags in the cupboards. I could hear the sound of footsteps on the stairs.

Dave didn't know I was in the kitchen and headed straight for the front room. I heard him shout, "Get up, you slag!"

This was quickly followed by a squeal of pain. It was clear that something bad was happening in the other room. In instances like this you get to discover something about yourself. I could've walked out the back door and away and no one would've known except for a drunken Dave. Even he might not've remembered, given the state he was in. I could've snuck into the back of the church and pretended what was happening in that house was nothing to do with me.

I make many bad decisions in my life; I don't say that in the past tense because each day is a struggle to make good choices and, like you, I don't always get it right. However, that day, I turned in the right direction. I hurried towards the front room; the door was wide open and Janine was lying on her front on the sofa. Her head was pulled back at what must've been a painful angle. Dave had grabbed a fistfull of hair and yanked up with his left hand, and was repeatedly striking her face and head with his right hand.

I rushed forward and grabbed hold of him but couldn't break his grip. I was worried that if I pulled him too hard, Janine's neck might be permanently damaged. Stepping back, I punched at the back of Dave's neck, where it joined his shoulders. I pivoted at the hips and put a great deal of force into the blow. Smack! He released Janine, who fell forward onto the sofa. Dave was momentarily stunned, but, regaining composure, he turned round and swung wildly at me. He was drunk and telegraphing his blows, by which I mean he was pulling his arm back too far each time he tried a punch and swinging too wildly. His movements were grossly exaggerated, allowing me to fend off most of his blows and step out of the way of the rest. However, this could not continue indefinitely. This struggle went as many stand-up fights do, to the ground. He grabbed hold of the front of my jacket and, in trying to break the grip, we both fell to the ground and wrestled for top mount position. I managed to prevail, before rolling sideways and up to show that I didn't want to hurt him. This allowed him to stand up; he approached me aggressively, with evident violent intent.

I shouted, "Stop! Dave, we're smashing your house up, you can't want that." As lame as it sounded, it was all I could think of.

"We aren't going to stop till we found out who's the best man!" Dave wasn't being placated.

"We can settle this without smashing your house up, Dave," I offered, as I fended off a blow.

He stopped and looked puzzled. "What do you mean, what are you on about?"

"Let's have an arm wrestle; whoever wins will be the best man. We can sort that out without wrecking your front room."

As he stood swaying, he looked down at the floor, taking in the upturned coffee table, and then turned his gaze back to me. Silence. Punctuated only by my heavy breathing and Janine's sobs. Clumsily, he got to his knees and righted the coffee table. He put his right elbow on the table and said, "Come on then, let's see who's best."

Now I don't pretend to be the strongest or toughest man you'll meet, but I'd been working out. With European Union funding, the youth service had been able to open our youth club in the daytime. There was a mother and toddlers' group, sessions for the unemployed, weight-loss groups and, most relevant for this situation, a basic gym, with free weights and a weight machine for bench presses, chess presses and lat pulldowns.

It'd be very rare for me to miss a session. Dave on the other hand, although bigger in build than me, only lifted the weight of several pint glasses on an average day.

As we took the strain, Dave attempted a sly quick attack, but I was ready for it and managed to hold on as he pushed, pushed again and strained. I began to feel him tire, but held on longer, just to be sure. As he flagged, I pushed down with all my strength, banging his fist onto the surface of the table and twisting him towards the floor in the process. We both stood up, massaged our right arms and faced each other.

"It's not over yet!" Dave exclaimed. I thought this meant the fighting would continue. "Back down. Time for the left arm."

I knelt down, relieved and a little bit more confident. Although I'm right-handed, unusually my left arm is stronger than my right. I nearly lost my left arm in a childhood accident, and after obsessive physiotherapy and endlessly repeated grip exercises, my left pectoral muscle is much larger than my right.

The outcome was never in doubt. Within a few seconds I'd won. We rose to our feet, and Dave spit into his open palm and extended his hand to me. "I give best. Here is my hand, here is my heart."

The handshake was uncomfortable to say the least. It was the second time I had to endure such a gesture. Making a mental note to wash my hand as soon as I could, I said, "No, Dave, you're the best man in your own home."

"Right, now that's over with, I'm off back to church," said Dave matter-of-factly. He brushed passed me and headed towards the back door. A desperate and destructive environment for a fractured family of four to exist in.

Stopping for a few seconds, I tried to weigh up what I ought to do. Should I stay and try to find out if Janine was alright, or should I follow Dave and stop him interrupting the worship again?

"Janine are you okay?" I asked.

"I am now that bastard's gone," she spat in reply.

"What are you going to do? Is there someone you can go and stay with?" I was concerned about her safety.

"I can take the kids with me to me Mam's," she said. "But I'll be back tomorrow."

"But why put up with it?" I asked. "I mean, no one should have to face that."

I suppose I'd just witnessed a familiar occurrence for Janine. I couldn't understand how anyone would want to continue in such an abusive relationship. It seemed as if she was reaching the same conclusion as me.

"I've just about done with him anyway," she said.

Thinking that Janine would take herself and the children off to her mother's house, I headed out the door and jogged towards the church, hoping to catch up with Dave before he got to the door.

He was almost at the churchyard gate when I stopped him with a tap on the shoulder.

"Now Dave, you know I can't let you go back into church," I said, with a conviction I didn't feel.

I thought we'd established the pecking order and he'd follow my instruction. However, all the talk of "giving best" counted for nothing in that instant. Pulling back his right fist he said, "You've just made a big mistake." Over his shoulder I could see people beginning to leave. The service was over.

"Dave, you can go on if it means that much to you," I said, relieved.

I accompanied him into the back of the church as people chatted and got ready to leave. He made his way down towards the front, down to the right side where the Lady Chapel altar was. Getting on his knees he bowed his head, closed his eyes and started to pray.

That was two weeks previously; now I was approaching Dave, golf club in hand, wondering how it would go. As we drew near I said out of the side of my mouth, "Tristan. Drop behind me and get ready to run. Last time I saw this bloke we had a fight."

As I got within a few feet of him I raised my hand in greeting. "How do Dave. How's it going?" I said, trying to sound calm and even.

"Alright Seth. How do."

We passed each other as if the incident had never happened and, relieved, I headed for home.

Dave and Janine, however, did not split up. The abuse carried on. Janine had suffered for many years as a child, enduring in silence what no child should have to, as foul offence after offence was committed.

And now as an adult the cycle was continuing. Her children were locked into an abusive situation, which came to a head a few weeks later, when Janine's toddler daughter was horribly burned.

According to the local paper, Janine blamed Dave. However, witnesses proved that Janine was at fault, and she subsequently confessed to the police. The little girl has been throwing a tantrum which reached such a pitch that she could no longer cope with. Janine grabbed for her, held her down, reached for a hot fire poker and plunged it into the desperate child's cheek.

She denied inflicting grievous bodily harm with intent against her daughter, but the jury found her guilty and in sentencing, the judge declared, "What you did was a wicked and unnatural act."

The brother and sister were taken into foster care, while Janine was taken into custody. She served nine months of her one-year sentence in a large women's prison in London. She was awarded three months remission for good behavior and released into the care of her family. She had no chance to rehabilitate, to atone for her sins, to change her ways and make amends. Within a year she suffered a massive heart attack and died where she fell.

Some people saw a measure of natural justice in this tragedy, but not me. I felt sick, sick that I hadn't done more to help the family. I reasoned they weren't on my patch, I'd enough on my plate, what with the needs of my flock at Bluebell Common. Hadn't I stopped her from getting a hiding? Hadn't I urged her to leave? Despite my inner dialogue, despite the reasoning, I still felt I'd let her and her children down.

The power of social media has allowed me to snoop and discover a little of what subsequently happened to the family. It's hard to find any light shining in the darkness of this situation. However, I did find Janine's daughter online, and she appears to be living a happy life with a good job. Sometimes it takes the worst of situations to bring out the best in people.

Chapter 13

I WILL NOT KILL THIS MAN

There are times when I reflect on an incident and just can't make sense of what took place. I understand what happened physically, of course, but the why or the wherefore is sometimes beyond me. I try to be as truthful to myself as possible when recollecting incidents I was party to, but even when you share an experience with someone, their recollection of what took place can be far removed from your own.

I'm a different person to the young man I was 30 years ago, to the naive 23-year-old who accepted the post at Bluebell Common and experienced so much. I don't think I'm any better; I'm convinced that I'm still a work in progress with many flaws, but I am more experienced and have taken more than my fair share of knocks. When I mull over the time when a stranger tried his best to ignore the voices telling him to kill me, I view it through the lens of nearly three decades of life experience and am sure there's a rational explanation. However, at the time, I was convinced that I was engaged in raw, supernatural spiritual warfare. I believed that a battle was raging against dark forces, and if I didn't keep my guard up, then I too could be attacked or even find myself possessed.

This incident has worried me over the years. It's almost as if the man concerned emerged from a sea of broken humanity, and, as quickly as he emerged, the waves parted and he was swallowed again and lost to me. I sometimes wonder what happened to him, whether he found the sanctuary he was seeking.

Under the banner of a loose affiliation of congregations known as 'Our Churches Together', a colleague was hosting a special service. The speaker was a self-proclaimed archbishop, supposedly a miracle worker in his own country. *We'll see*, I thought. He'd published an impressive book detailing some of the miracles God would allow you to perform if you tapped into his mighty power.

Having been brought up in a charismatic, evangelical Christian family where miracles were to be expected, I knew what this meeting would probably be like. I'd experienced first hand the false promises and dashed expectations which frequently surrounded such events.

In the past, I'd watched closely as a man with a healing ministry had prayed for my younger brother; one of his legs grew by at least an inch before my eyes. This was supposedly God healing a pain in his hip from a sporting injury he picked up whilst competing at county-level shot-put. I've since seen how anyone can replicate this with a simple trick; a quick search online will lead you to videos exposing this technique.

Vague illnesses, bad backs, migraines and other hard-to-diagnose maladies were frequently claimed to be healed at such gatherings. As the adrenaline flows and endorphins kick in during exuberant worship, people may feel temporary relief from even chronic pain. I've never seen an amputated limb or even a little finger grow back at any of these gatherings. Writing this has reminded me of an ironic exchange with a colleague, who claimed to have witnessed a limb growing back during a healing service; ironic because the next day this colleague developed a sore throat and had a whole week off work. Apparently God was in the business of restoring missing limbs, but a sore throat was just too much for him to deal with.

I didn't want to attend the meeting, but felt that I should support my colleague and the fledgling umbrella organisation. So I decided that I would go myself, but not take any of my small congregation with me.

This miracle service followed a familiar pattern: a warm welcome, then an opening prayer giving way to exuberant worship; guitars, keyboard and drums leading the up-tempo singing of some old classic hymns and new worship songs.

I'd sat at the back of the church, more of an observer than a participator, but even I could feel the wave of enthusiasm and anticipation building in this emotionally charged atmosphere.

As the singing continued, the door to the church flew open, and in staggered a clearly drunk man. He appeared to be anxious, looking over his shoulder as he entered.

Here comes trouble, I thought. He grabbed the heavy door with both hands and slammed it shut. One of the wardens seated at the rear of the church stepped forward, and after what appeared to be a heated conversation, he tried to steer the man towards the door.

I left my seat to join in the struggle and offer support. As the song continued, fortunately drowning out much of the noise of the tussle, the man expressed a desire – no, a need – to be inside a church.

He was clearly scared and thought that the church building would provide some sanctuary from whatever was pursuing him. Thinking fast, as the song reached its conclusion, I decided to follow my standard operating procedure for drunks disturbing a church service (most frequently during Midnight Mass at Christmas) by getting him away from the building as soon as possible, minimising the disturbance for the majority of those present. We managed to hustle him out to the church steps and closed the door behind us.

"You don't understand," he pleaded. "I have to be inside a church." He seemed genuinely agitated.

"Well, you can't come in and disturb it for everyone else," the churchwarden insisted.

The man appeared to be desperate and we were at an impasse.

"I have a chapel in my house. I can take you there and then we can talk," I suggested.

The man looked desperate; he gazed at the warden standing between him and the door, weighing up his chances. I could see that he was struggling to come to a decision. He deferred to my suggestion and followed me to my car. I thought that I could kill two birds with one stone, by removing the man from the church and preventing a possible scene, and also removing myself from a service I hadn't really wanted to attend in the first place.

As we pulled away and onto the access road to the church, I explained to him that it was a 15-minute drive from my house, and the chapel. I told him who I was, that although I didn't have a dog collar on, I was a minister of the church, and the front room of my house was a small chapel, a blessed place of worship.

He seemed to have calmed down, and as we drove north up the dual carriageway towards my village, he visibly relaxed.

"You seemed a little bit frightened back there," I said. "Don't get me wrong, I was frightened. But when we get into your church, I'll show you a radiance you won't believe." He faced me as he said this and I could smell alcohol on his breath, but could make no sense of what I'd just heard. His words were bizarre to say the least and left me feeling unnerved.

We drove the rest of the way in silence; I didn't know how to respond to what he'd said and he offered no more explanation.

I played back the sequence of events in my mind as I drove. His entry into church, his unsteady gait, his looking over his shoulder into the dark of the night, his smile of satisfaction at the slammed-shut church door. Was he running from someone, or something? His unusual statement seemed so offbeat, so strange, that I couldn't relax.

As we parked and got out of the car, I asked him to walk round to the front door while I entered the house through the back door and bolted the door that separated the chapel from the rest of the building. I don't know why I did that, but I felt that I needed to. I retraced my steps, locking the back door and joined him at the front door to the chapel. Unlocking it, we walked in and I invited him to sit down on one of the wooden church seats. I asked what he wanted to do; he replied that he was content to be there and he just wanted to pray. He bowed his head but remained silent. After a while he looked up and said, "I feel safe now. It's going to be alright."

I pushed my misgivings to one side and reasoned to myself that here was nothing more than a troubled soul, seeking the answer to his problems in the bottom of a bottle and finding nothing there, like all those who'd previously tried this remedy. He'd clearly derived some comfort from being in the chapel, and from his prayers.

"Would you like me to pray for you?" I asked.

"No, we would not," he intoned, in a forceful but quiet voice.

I instinctively recoiled at these words: almost a reflex action, like jumping back from an oncoming speeding car.

"It's time to go," he said.

I suddenly realised how stupid I'd been. Here I was, alone and without support, with a drunken, possibly mentally ill, perhaps even demonised man. What did he mean by "no we would not" in response to my offer of prayer? Again, an offbeat statement had disturbed me, setting me on the back foot. One thing was clear: whatever was happening here, I didn't have an answer. I needed help, and I needed the safety in numbers that returning to the church would give me.

We left Church House and entered my car without incident. I felt anxious and now wanted to return to the service I was so reluctant to attend earlier. I don't know if my demeanor or body language communicated my unease to the man, but I was aware that something felt different. My senses had sharpened and I was ready for something to happen.

As we headed south along the dual carriageway, towards the centre of town, the man jerked upright in his seat.

I WILL NOT KILL THIS MAN

"No! I will not kill this man!" He spoke loudly at an unseen presence. I didn't know whether this was just the ramblings of a drunk and sick man, or something more sinister, but I felt a basic, instinctive fear.

"I will not grab that steering wheel!" he barked, as his right hand streaked out and grabbed it. At this point I was driving at around 45 miles per hour and I'd noticed a marked police car in my rearview mirror that had joined the road at the last roundabout.

I tried to break his grip, but couldn't. Thankfully he wasn't attempting to turn the wheel to the left or the right, and the carriageway was running straight.

I shouted words that just seemed to come into my head; it was almost as if I wasn't saying them, but they were being pulled out of my mouth. "In the name of Jesus, I command you to release this steering wheel!" This provoked an instant reaction; he pulled his hand back and looked at it as if it'd been scalded.

"They are telling me that I have to kill you," he informed me. In that instant I remembered Dennis's words to me all those weeks before: "We hate Seth Walker. We can't get him because his faith is too strong, but he can trip himself up." Had I tripped myself up here by acting on my own? I'd been foolish and was in over my head. I started to feel nauseous as fear began to take over. If I didn't make an effort to react rationally, I'd be in danger of giving in to this spreading fear, and who knows what would've happened then.

As I thought about this, the police car pulled alongside and then sped off into the distance. Now I *was* frightened: I was alone, miles from help, in my car with I didn't know what. I wondered whether I should flash my lights to attract the police car's attention – surely they could help? But what would I say, how could I explain what was happening in a way that would make sense? I thought that involving the police at that point would do more harm than good, and may well have seen both of us as residents of the local psychiatric ward.

"Have you got a cigarette lighter?" the man asked. "Where is it?"

I had one – in those days they came as standard on all cars – but I wasn't going to tell him that.

"They're telling me that I need to burn you," he said. Whether he was just drunk and playing a sick game, mentally ill or under demonic control was a moot point. Whatever was behind his behaviour, the threat to me was real and concrete. I still had to deal with the situation, on my own, in the dark of the night, whilst driving my vehicle and fighting back against a wave of terror.

The journey to the church was not a quick one, and was punctuated by statements from the man about what the voices were telling him to do, along with prayers from me, prayers to take authority over whatever was causing his bizarre behaviour.

After what seemed like an age, we arrived back at the church. The man refused to leave the car. When I tried to open the passenger door, he clutched the handle from the inside, held his arm rigid and shouted again, "I will not kill this man!"

After a tense minute, he stepped out of the car and explained to me that he was being told to shut my head in the car door.

This time, when the church door was flung open, it wasn't by a drunken man, but by me. I steered us towards the vestry at the back of the church, motioning to the churchwarden to come with us. As we entered the vestry, the man looked out of the window and shouted, "You can't come in here, you bastards!"

I asked the churchwarden, who was far from impressed that I had brought this drunk man back to his church to disturb the service, to be quiet and listen. I asked him to go into the church and quickly bring back three people I named, who I knew had experience in the deliverance ministry, to take over from me.

I wasn't entirely comfortable with what followed, but I needed help and had to accept it in any form. As these men prayed with him, he writhed as he sat on a pew that ran along the side wall of the vestry. It seemed as if unseen hands were pushing him along the pew. The atmosphere was fearful, with prayers from us and shouting and swearing from the man. Finally, after the demons had supposedly been cast out, he slumped, relieved. The sense of fear had gone; only a drunken man remained. A young colleague and I drove the man back to his flat, made a note of his address and said we would call round in the morning.

The next morning he had no recollection of who we were or what had taken place. He knew he'd been drunk and had attempted to come to church, but didn't know why; he certainly didn't want any involvement from his local church. As we left his flat, I handed him over to the care of my colleague, who worked this parish. I never saw or heard from him again.

Had I tripped myself up as Dennis had warned? Perhaps I'd made a mistake, but thankfully I am still here to tell the tale. It isn't always possible to have a chaperone when you minister; life isn't always so ordered or neat. When you deal with those who lead chaotic lives, you have to make the best of bad situations. If I had my time again, I wouldn't have left the church on my own with this man. Thankfully, he didn't have the chance to obey his voices; in fact he stood up to them and we both emerged relatively unharmed. I had learnt an important lesson: this was the last time I gave a lift to a stranger.

Chapter 14

JANE AND THE SEVEN-FOOT BIKER

Jane was a single parent. She was a prime example of those young women who were being demonised in some of the right-wing press: a single parent, with no partner on the scene to offer help or financial support. Worse still, she had no job, and, like 64 per cent of the households in Bluebell Common, her life was blighted by unemployment. The popular reggae band UB40 had recently charted with a hit song entitled 'I am a one in ten', the statistic relating to the national unemployment rate at that time. At Bluebell Common it was more like 'We are the six in ten.'

The village had originally been built to house migrant miners from the north-east and Scottish coalfields. Along with their families, this meant that around 2,000 people originally lived there. With the demand for coal soaring, and the limitless supply of a seam as tall as a bus and stretching five miles towards Brinsley, it seemed that a job down the pit was a job for life. However, the vagaries of the free market would mean that this home-grown industry would be hamstrung by unfair competition from abroad. Our industry couldn't compete with coal from the Eastern Bloc, supposedly dug by prisoners for free. It was a blow that our coalfields couldn't recover from; the Bradley pit closed just 18 months after the bitter year-long miners' strike, the hardship endured by the whole community as they fought to keep the pits open compounded when the colliery closed its gates for the last time. The strike had done nothing to enable the pits to stay open; if anything it had sped up their demise.

The strike had driven the wedge between the community and the police force deeper, going some way to explain what most people would see as unreasonable hostility and deep-seated distrust.

During the strike, police officers were bused into the village, some from as far away as London. I heard tales of policemen opening their tunics to show T-shirts saying, "Thanks for paying for my conservatory", referring to the generous overtime they earned during the dispute. Ex-miners would say to me, "If Maggie could afford all those police, she could afford to pay us a decent wage and keep the pits open."

I heard one tale, possibly apocryphal, but worth relating here, because it illustrates the divide between the people of the village and the forces of law and order. More than that, it also shows what forward planning, comrades working together and a sense of humour can achieve.

The winter of the strike was at times a bitter one, with snowfall not uncommon. As a transit van full of police officers patrolled the village streets, a group of men emerged from an alleyway, at the head of which stood a snowman they'd built, complete with coal buttons and topped with a toy police helmet. The men were armed with snowballs, which they flung with venom at the van. The policemen were in no mood to let this go and turned the van round as the culprits ran off towards the alleyway. The van sped on in pursuit. I don't know why, but the driver saw the snowman and thought that if they couldn't catch the perpetrators, they could at least smash their creation. I was told that the van must have been travelling at 30 miles an hour when it hit the snowman. The collision damaged the police van beyond repair. It was a write off, fit only for scrap, and had to be recovered by a tow truck.

These police officers, brought in from a far-off county, didn't know that the striking miners had built the snowman around a concrete bollard. They had been lured into a trap. They'd taken the bait, and in their haste to seek some revenge for the childish snowball attack, had fallen for a well-planned prank; the morale of the village was lifted for a short while.

The demise of the pit ripped the heart out of the village. Those who could got jobs elsewhere and left the village. Tradesmen, engineers, electricians and mechanics with skills to offer slowly migrated to wherever jobs could be found. As the houses became vacant, the council were struggling to fill them. Who would come to an isolated village with no offer of local employment?

Those who were desperate was the answer. A social worker I collaborated with told me that the village had the shortest waiting list for housing in the whole of the metropolitan borough. This is some indication of the level of depravation that had taken hold. A once thriving, vibrant and happy village had been driven to its knees and abandoned.

Jane had moved to the village as a teenager with her family; they had nowhere else to go.

As time wore on, she found herself running with Billy's crew. Slowly but surely, she found herself drawn into their web of chaos. When they broke into my predecessor's house, Jane and Tony made their way to the main bedroom where they did what comes naturally. That incident, which lasted for just a few moments, had an impact that would stay with her for the rest of her life. Jane fell pregnant.

For a while she had no idea that she had 'caught', and she continued her usual lifestyle. When her little son was two, Jane told me that he'd been conceived in what was to become my bed. This for me was one of the overheads of ministering in the village: there were no secrets and no sanctuary. Even my most private room was known to the crew. More than that, it had been used for a loveless, lustful act; a few moments' release from the mundane, monochrome existence of life on the dole.

This knowledge was like water torture for me, drip by drip, my privacy being eroded and my strength sapped. As I look back at my time in service to the church, I think it was the knowledge of what had happened in my bed, nearly two years before I arrived, that kicked off the process that would lead to my crisis of faith. It disturbed me at the time, but, as on most days, I smiled and carried on, with one more straw on my back.

Jane was present for what proved to be the last straw for my predecessor. The following account is an amalgamation of what three people, two who were actually there, have told me.

It was just another night, when, bored and looking for action, the crew met up with Billy. He had a gas canister and was looking for somewhere to get out of his head. Someone else had scored some acid; they had the ingredients for a party, now all they needed was a venue. Someone had suggested Church House, and the crew turned and walked up the street as one. It wasn't late, around nine o'clock, but the lights were off. Billy used his cat-like agility to climb up onto the single-storey kitchen roof. Leaning across, he grabbed and rattled the bedroom window until it opened.

He'd done this several times before and knew that the loose catch would eventually spring from its housing and allow him to enter.

As he slithered into the bedroom, he became aware that the room was indeed occupied. My predecessor, exhausted by the burdens of ministry, had sought some rest through an early night.

"You can stay there," Billy ordered, as he headed downstairs to open the door and let the crew in.

Jane told me they carried on partying downstairs whilst my predecessor attempted to rest. She explained that it'd happened before and he was too frightened to do anything about it. She told me they'd sniffed glue and dropped acid before someone suggested they take it further. They'd constructed a rudimentary ouija board out of scraps of paper, and, using glasses from the kitchen, they attempted to communicate with the 'other side'.

As a skeptic I don't believe they called anything up, but in that emotionally charged, substance-fuelled moment, they'd bypassed the usual moral constraints and embarked on a collective folly that could have resulted in tragedy. I've watched videos which show mediums using ouija boards to good effect, spelling out names and answering questions. The glass appears to be under the control of a spirit force as it speeds around the alphabet. When the same 'mediums' are blindfolded and the board is turned upside down, the glass, under their fingers, once again speeds round the board.

This time of course it misses the letters and an unintelligible message is received. The same result happens no matter how many times the experiment is carried out. There can only be one conclusion: even if the players believe they're communicating with spirits, they're not. They're fooling themselves.

Jane told me matter-of-factly about the events of that night, as described in the opening chapter. I later heard the tale from Billy's point of view, but it was Jane's retelling that upset me the most. When they had dragged the minister from his bed, bathed him in cold water, tied him to a chair, beat him and then psychologically broke him, someone suggested they burn him. A blanket was fetched and draped over his head, and, according to Jane, they found a bottle of white spirit under the sink and emptied it onto the blanket over his head. Jane told me she had a disposable lighter in her hand and flicked the wheel to ignite the flame. She was then slowly moving her hand towards the figure slumped in the chair when a series of loud knocks on the living room window disturbed her progress.

She describes it like a spell being broken. She said everybody collectively shook their heads and looked at each other, and she said, "What the fuck have we done?!"

Now, as a single parent, she was trapped. Who'd want to swap with her? There was no exchange of housing available to her, so there she would stay.

I'd previously asked whether dad was on the scene, but although he was still in the village, he didn't play a meaningful part in Jane's or her son's lives. This was the reality for her. Day in, day out, life on benefits, with a carbon-copy son ready to keep the cycle of depravation going.

That day I'd contemplated walking on past Jane's house, but knowing she was overdue a visit, I decided to knock and see if she was in. She was tough, as broad as she was tall – and could well handle herself if needed. I would rather face Billy than her if it came to a fight. I knew she was troubled by her involvement in the incident with my predecessor; she felt remorse and, tough as she was, I felt she wasn't too far from becoming part of our little flock. She attended the mother and toddlers' group at the youth club and we'd spoken together about faith and what it could offer her. Perhaps this visit would be another step on her journey into faith?

Jane lived in a three-bedroomed terraced house similar to mine, the only difference being that hers was the centre of a block of three and mine was an end house. I rapped on the living room window as I walked to the back door, which was how we all let people know they had company on our street. Almost immediately there was a visible disturbance of the net curtains, an indication someone was close to the window and trying to see who was there. As I got to the door I heard a rattle as the door chain was disengaged and the mechanical clunk of a bolt being withdrawn. Now this was unusual. Jane was afraid of no one. Something must've been badly wrong for her to hide behind a locked door. She opened the door, looked over my shoulder and motioned for me to come in. I complied, knowing this would be an interesting visit. As I got through the door, she slammed it shut, turned the key in the lock, drew the chain and closed the bolt. Something was indeed wrong.

We entered her lounge and I got a good look at her. Her neck was red and marked and there was a swelling under her left eye.

"What's happened?" I asked, as calmly as I could.

"I'm shitting meself," was her opening remark. "I've just been beat up by a seven-foot biker and he says he's coming back to finish the job." *Oh, great*! I thought. What was I going to do?

"See my neck?" she asked as she lifted her chin up for me to examine her injury, "He strangled me with one hand. That's all it took, one hand. His hands are like fucking bunches of bananas."

She was clearly agitated, frightened and at her wit's end.

"Let's have a cup of tea and you can tell me all about it," I suggested. I hoped that getting her to perform this routine task would help her to calm down, to give her another focus, whilst I thought the situation through.

I didn't believe that the man was seven-foot tall for one minute, but he must've been big and powerfully built to subdue Jane. Her 'go to' move was a head butt; once this was delivered with her mass behind it, there was usually little need for anything else. Her assailant had demonstrated some impressive skills to beat her. Also, he had done enough to make her fear his return, indicating he was no mug.

She told me that he was an outlaw biker, a member of one of the big two clubs, I doubted this was true; for most people, a leather jacket and a big motorcycle is enough for someone to be labeled a 'Hells Angel', but nothing could be further from the truth. An American motorcycle association estimated in the 1960s that 1 per cent of all bikers were outlaws, and the Angels, although arguably the most powerful of outlaw clubs, made up only a fraction of that 1 per cent. In the United Kingdom during the late 1980s the outlaw biker scene was going through a time of rapid change, as smaller clubs were 'patched over' and subsumed into the larger clubs. There were probably less than 400 Angels in the country, divided into 10 Chapters. At that time, the nearest Chapter was based near Nottingham. The likelihood of Jane, an outsider to the world of outlaw bikers, meeting up with a club member was remote.

"So," I began. "Do you want to tell me about it?"

"I've been seeing him for a while," she explained. "He's been good to me and given me money to spend on the little one. But I don't fancy him. He flies off the handle at the smallest thing. I lost my rag with him and he did this to me." She indicated her neck. "He says he's coming back to finish it off." At this she started to cry. It was hard to take in. Jane never cried; she had rarely smiled during our interactions either.

"Can't you go and stay with your mum until it all blows over?" I suggested.

"No chance. I can't bring her into this, he knows where she lives. She's got Dan, I don't want her seeing me getting the shit kicked out of me again." Jane had resigned herself to her fate. She had no support and was on her own. She definitely couldn't call the police. She had enough of a mother's protective instinct to keep her son out of harm's way, and was waiting to take her licks.

"I'll stay here and sit with you," I offered.

"What do you mean, you'll stop here with me?" she asked, puzzled. "What are you going to do? He's seven foot tall, he'll kill you."

She had a point. I was no fighter. I was five foot ten and 160 pounds. However, I knew from experience that most threats of future harm were without substance. A drunken man once told me to keep looking over my shoulder because he would get me. He said this in his front room as he swigged cheap whisky and cola from a tumbler, playing the big man in front of his family. That was the last I ever saw of him and the threat came to nothing. I was pretty certain that Jane's biker wouldn't return. Pretty certain, but not completely convinced. Good point Jane: what would I do?

"I'll talk to him. That's what I do. I talk to people," was my lame reply. I'm sure I didn't sound convincing; I was far from convinced myself, but what else could I do? I could unbolt, unchain, unlock the door and go home. But I couldn't leave Jane in her hour of need, could I?

As we sat, shooting the breeze, drinking endless cups of tea whilst Jane chain-smoked roll-ups, I thought about the why, not the what.

Why was I there? I'm used to questioning myself. I'd been trained by years of evangelical Christianity to take the blame for anything I might have done wrong or that hadn't gone as well as it could have, whilst giving any credit for my few successes to God. This double blow to your self-esteem, this liberal application of the stick combined with a denial of carrot, is one of the factors that helped me walk through the door and into the light of atheism. I'm more than happy to take responsibility when I get it wrong, but I'm now ready to take pride and a sense of achievement when I get it right and not offer it all to God, who seems too busy organising a global plague, or a tsunami the day after his son's birthday, to be bothered anyway.

There I was, sitting with an assault victim, waiting for a confrontation with a violent man, and I was questioning why I was there. I was even thinking it was because I didn't want Jane to think I was a coward. How deep was I sunk into the I was actually there trumped any bad motive? In those days it wasn't enough for me to do the right thing, I had to do the right thing for the right motive. Looking back, I'm proud I sat there with Jane. I don't care why I was there; the fact is, I was.

I wasn't sure what I'd do when or if he returned, or even what I'd say. I'd think of something; I always seemed to.

As the minutes passed into hours, darkness began to fall. It became increasingly clear he wasn't returning. He never did. Another empty threat, designed to sow fear, delivered by a supposedly seven-foot-tall man, but who was nevertheless a small man inside.

As I said goodbye and headed up the street to my house, I had the feeling that Jane now owed me. I'd waited with her in her time of need, giving me a chip I'd be able to cash in when the time was right. It might just be the leverage that would get her to a church service, that just might begin her journey of faith.

I'd been holding a series of small-scale events designed to bring in people who wouldn't usually attend Church House. A rock drummer, who had played with some of the most successful bands of the time and had previously worked with me in London and Lancashire, came to tell his story; a former gangland enforcer told his powerful testimony of a journey from a life of crime and violence to forgiveness, love and acceptance. Jane didn't come to either of these meetings, but I called in my marker with her when a man my father had worshipped with 20 years earlier came to speak.

He bought a worship team with him. The worship songs were emotionally charged. As he spoke, a sense of expectation filled the room. The music started again as he moved around praying for people, delivering messages from God, speaking words of release to those imprisoned by their sin.

Jane remained in her seat. When the service was over I desperately tried to engineer a meeting between her and the speaker but she'd have none of it,

"He's full of shit," was all she'd say. In the end, however, one of my parishioners introduced the man to Jane. Five minutes of intense prayer, shouting, and, according to the man, deliverance, followed, as he attempted to rid her of all evil spiritual influence. When he finished, she seemed to be at peace. I thought perhaps we'd made a breakthrough and she'd become a convert.

It wasn't to be. At a follow-up visit, despite feeling the benefit of the prayer, she stuck to her former opinion of him and refused to attend any more meetings. So near and yet so far. I had called in the favour owed with no result: it was an opportunity wasted, or was it?

Looking back, Jane's life was entwined with the work of the church at Bluebell Common; her son was conceived in Church House, she was part of the reason for my predecessor's demise and I'd hoped that she could become part of our congregation. It wasn't to be.

I'm convinced some good came of it, even if it was just the knowledge that at her time of greatest need, she found out that someone was willing to sit with her and face the potential of a beating along with her. I gained two valuable lessons which have stayed with me: the first is that perhaps motives do not always matter if there's a tangible benefit. Remember the ethic of the lesser of two evils? Which was worse, that I sat and waited with her because my motives were questionable, or that I left, only to return when my motives were 100 per cent right, and she'd suffered alone?

The other learning point was that sometimes it's enough just to be there. She was alone, frightened and had resigned herself to a further beating. Sitting and waiting alone would have been an unbearable experience. The anticipation of harm and the fear that would have tormented her would have done her considerable emotional harm if faced alone. We don't always know what people are going through, but we can be there with them in the midst of their suffering, to let them know they're not on their own.

Chapter 15

BILLY WANTS TO KILL ME

Billy is the elder of two children. Along with his younger brother Steve, he was amongst the toughest of the young people in the village. Neither of them lasted the course at school. Billy's education was cut short by a stretch in Borstal. He told me it was for grievous bodily harm, carried out on four men at the same time. I don't know the truth of that statement, but I once witnessed his fighting prowess and was physically attacked by him on another occasion, so I believe it's plausible.

When you're unemployed, living in a household where no one works, barely existing on benefits, tempers sometimes fray as the pressure of daily living builds. On one particular occasion, brotherly bonds were stretched to breaking point. I don't know what had caused the argument, but it wasn't to be solved by reason or words.

Billy and Steve were facing off against each other in the middle of North Street, stripped to the waist with fists held either side of their faces.

Steve was shorter but stockier and heavily muscled. Billy was taller, lithe, without an ounce of visible fat. As they exchanged blows, shouts from the crowd of onlookers punctuated the action.

The fight didn't last long, however. Whether in response to a call (which was unlikely on our estate) or whether by pure chance, a police patrol car arrived.

The policemen exited the vehicle and, as I stepped outside into my backyard, Steve went racing past me. Billy wasn't quick enough, however; he was wrestled to the ground, his hands cuffed behind his back and he was thrown into the rear of the police car. The police aren't daft and know the score, so they made a hasty retreat in the face of a lively crowd. The action now over, people started to return to what they'd been doing. Before long the street was nearly empty again.

I returned to my kitchen to make a cup of tea: just another episode of happy families in the lost world of Bluebell Common. Half an hour later I left my house and walked down the road to visit a member of our congregation, the matriarch of a large family that lived on the estate. But before I reached her house, I noticed a bedraggled figure limping up the street, a young man. He was topless and had obviously been beaten. He had a bloodied, bruise and scraped body. It was Billy. I went to help him but he pushed me away, heading towards his family's house.

"What happened Billy?" I asked, clearly concerned.

"The bastards took me to the industrial estate, pulled me out of the car with the cuffs on and beat the shit out of me. Then they undid me and let me go," he spat. "Still, I managed to dig one in the ribs when they took the cuffs off." He chuckled, winced, then made his way home.

Billy was a likeable rogue, with an in-built need to be wanted and accepted. During daytime sessions at the youth club, we struck up a rapport as we lifted weights and played pool.

Billy ran with a small crew who were involved in petty crime and occasionally chanced their arm at something more serious.

One enterprise saw them calling themselves the Bluebell Common Coal Board. This involved running alongside slow-moving coal trucks pulled by a diesel locomotive train that ran near the village. As they jogged alongside, they turned a wheel that lifted up a metal plate, emptying hundreds of tons of coal alongside the railway track. They'd then collect it with stolen shovels and wheelbarrows, bag it and attempt to sell it door-to-door. It was a type of coal destined for a power station and not for domestic use but it still lit and gave off good heat.

I became aware of the activities of the Bluebell Common Coal Board when one of my parishioners asked me to have a word with them. They would cold-call prospective customers at night, dressed in black with balaclavas covering everything except their eyes. Older residents found this intimidating, as did my parishioners.

So I found myself for the second night in a row sitting in Lance's house, sipping tea and waiting for Billy and his crew to visit.

On the rare occasions when I have spoken about this incident with friends, people whose life experience is vastly different to the people of Bluebell Common, I have been met with a sense of disbelief. "But if someone had called the police in the first place, they'd have arrested them?" is a question I've heard several times. What people with no experience of the margins of the underworld don't appreciate is that there's an ethic, a code, that cannot be broken. The unwritten message that is indelibly burned on people's hearts is that *you do not grass*. Cooperation with the police was considered taboo.

An example of how embedded this tacit agreement was took place during my time with Davie. Davie was a cheerful, happy-go-lucky young man who attended our daytime sessions at the youth club. He was gregarious and warm-natured, but also a thief.

He'd been the chief suspect in a burglary during my first month at Bluebell Common. A pensioner's house had been broken into and a small amount of money, a radio and some jewellery had been taken. Although street whisperers were all in agreement that Davie was the culprit, nothing was said to the police.

Davie's activities did not always go unpunished, though. He was to learn the hard way that our actions have consequences, and sometimes those consequences can be terrible.

Davie had been at a friend's house when items of jewellery and some cash went missing. As usual, the police weren't called and the issue was dealt with using street justice. The householder and a male relative rounded Davie up, beat him and took him to a lock-up garage, where they tied him up, administered another beating and put his hand in a vice until the pain was excruciating. They burned his hand with a blowtorch and beat his legs with an iron bar. Davie was then taken in a car to the countryside, thrown onto a grass verge and left there.

This was not a regular occurrence, but it serves to illustrate the point that Bluebell Common people were often reluctant to talk to the police and would seek to deal with things their own way. And it was tough to argue it any other way.

When the knock came at Lance's door, my heart started to race. Lance and his wife were stalwarts of the church, and their active faith guided their life choices. They would not consider buying 'liberated' power-station coal, but were intimidated by the sales technique used by the Bluebell Common Coal Board. Although I knew the crew standing on his doorstep on a one-to-one basis – some would even say I was a friend – when they were all together, with their egos pushing them on and a mob mentality in the mix, I didn't know what would happen.

As I opened the door I was greeted by four individuals, darkly dressed and wearing balaclavas, but Billy, was clearly identifiable by build, voice and exposed tattoos.

"Hey up lads," I said, as friendly as I could manage. "How's it going?"

"Alright Seth. Is Lance there?" Billy said, then craned his neck to peer into the room.

"He is Billy, but to tell you the truth, now that he's a God-fearing man, his conscience won't let him buy coal from you."

"There is nowt wrong with this stuff, it's the best you can buy, and at a good price," Billy asserted.

"All the same Billy, if it's alright with you, Lance needs to follow what the good book says. He can't buy something that he knows has been knocked off. You do understand it's to do with his faith though, not you," I said.

"No problem Seth, we'll try next door," was Billy's reply.

"Thanks Billy, and one last thing," I asked. "Lance is a little bit worried. Can I tell him there will be no comebacks from this?"

"Oh no Seth, there'll be none of that. This is business and not personal."

With that, the small crew disappeared down the yard, pushing wheelbarrows full of the finest Bluebell Common Coal Board product.

Sometimes the best of intentions lead to the worst of all outcomes. Daniel was a professional man, a solicitor. He was also a man whose left-leaning politics had led him to open a small weekly surgery in the village. There was no reason why people with legal needs should find themselves abandoned just because the rest of society had turned their backs on them.

With legal aid paying the tab for most cases, and Daniel picking up the rest through pro-bono work, the surgery managed to limp on. To keep costs to a minimum, his teenage daughter sometimes helped out. It was here that his good intentions may well have been misplaced.

They say love is blind, and this was a case in point. His daughter, Celia, met Billy, who took a liking to her, and over the course of several meetings she began to fall in love with him.

Despite her parents' protestations and frequent admonitions, Celia kept seeing Billy and love blossomed. During her A-level year, she fell pregnant. Being stubborn, as some young girls can be, she was determined to keep the child and carry on seeing Billy. With their world crashing down around them, Daniel and his wife decided they'd do their best to provide for their grandchild, support their daughter and help the young couple.

Billy was encouraged to find a job, while Celia's parents set the couple up in a small house they'd purchased two miles from the village. For a short time, it looked as if they might even make it through. However, in a moment of post-natal clarity, Celia took a good look around her and realised the enormity of what she'd done. Whilst her friends were leaving for university, with careers beckoning, she was a young mother, in a relationship with a semi-literate petty criminal with a record for violence.

As their relationship became more and more strained, Billy found the reproaches from Celia's family harder and harder to stomach. The relationship, built on tentative foundations, fractured. Finally, Billy returned one day to what he thought was his home to find the locks changed and his belongings bundled onto the doorstep in black bin bags. Celia had taken the baby and fled to safety with her parents, leaving Billy on his own.

The rejection hit him hard. Leaving his belongings on the doorstep, he headed back towards Bluebell Common and hatched a plan.

It wasn't a very sophisticated plan; it had very few parts to it and would be simple to carry out. It just needed to be lubricated with several pints of Dutch courage if it was going to run smoothly.

I was unaware of this drama playing out in Billy's life. It was getting dark outside and I was getting ready to head out to attend a Pentecostal worship service in a farming community in North Yorkshire. I was scoping it out, hoping to take several other people to future events if it was suitable. The informal sense of worship and the supposed miracles performed in the name of the Lord might have more appeal than the more formal worship on offer in the parish church.

Standing in my lounge, I was trying to remember where I'd put my car keys when my thoughts were rudely interrupted by the noise and vibrations of a kick on my back door. It wasn't the sort of kick that someone might deliver if their arms were full and they were trying to mimic a knock. It was a full-on frame-blistering attempt to kick the door in. Looking through my net curtains, I could see Billy backing up and preparing for another run at the door.

He didn't look at all pleased. His face was frozen in a mask of anger and he seemed intent on his task.

Boom! The door vibrated in the frame but held; one more kick and the frame would surely splinter. Without thinking, I rushed to the back door to prevent Billy from breaking my door in, leaving the church with a large repair bill and my house insecure until it was fixed.

I fumbled the door open just as Billy began his third run-up. He looked at me and ran towards the doorway. I thought he was going to launch himself at me, but I stood my ground.

He pulled up just inches from me; I had a height advantage, with him a good six inches below me in the yard.

"Outside now you fucking twat," he spat at me. "Come on, I'm gonna kick your fucking head in!"

Oh dear, I thought. *This is not going to end very well.*

"Come on then! Get out here or am I gonna have to drag you out?"

"I'm not scared of you, Billy," I said, as evenly as I could, "and I am happy to fight you."

I was scared, tapping my feet to hide the shaking of my legs.

"But if you want to fight me, you can come inside where no one can see. I'm not going to lose my job over a scrap with you out in the street."

I wanted Billy to see that I wasn't showing weakness, but equally I didn't want to provoke him by being overly aggressive. If I stepped outside, the oxygen of the inevitable onlookers would quickly add fuel to the confrontation's fire. The situation would probably escalate, and even if I managed to hold my own against Billy, I'll still have his crew to deal with.

"Are you coming in?" I asked, as calmly as I could, and I stood to one side.

Billy pushed past me and moved into my lounge, taking up a fighting stance. I shut the back door and walked two steps into the room to face him.

Having seen Billy fight and heard tales of his violence, I was worried for my safety. But he was swaying on his feet, and the hoppy smell of his fetid booze breath reached me.

I didn't lift my fists to him, but held my hands up, with palms facing him, with my left hand closest to him. I didn't try to close the gap between us, but wanted this protective distance, this fence, to be there. I wanted him to be the one to decide to close the gap and start the fight.

Only he didn't attack me. He stared at me: a harsh, icy stare.

"Billy, before we do this, would you mind telling me what I've done?" I asked.

The question hung unanswered in the air between us. His eyes didn't leave mine.

"You keep telling me how good God is. What has he ever fucking done for me?" He jabbed his words at me.

"Billy," I replied, as evenly as I could manage. "What have you ever done for him?"

With that, he took two steps towards me and pulled his fist back to punch me. I stepped inside the blow and pushed him hard to the floor with both palms. While he was getting up I asked him again, "What have you ever done for God?"

And that was it: no more violence, just tears. Billy began to cry, sobbing, his chest heaving. I guided him to the sofa and sat him down, walked into the kitchen breathing a sigh of relief and filled the kettle. I returned with a handful of paper kitchen towels for him to wipe his face with. By the time the tea was made, he had begun to regain his composure and some of the old, cocky Billy was returning.

I had succeeded in taking Billy's fight out of him by opening the door instead of cowering from him and then standing my ground to maintain my height advantage, pushing him to the point of 'bottle drop'. Dictating the battleground, taking the initiative in inviting him in, all chipped away at his confidence. I'd stepped into his punch and pushed him with all my might; the fight was over without a proper blow being landed.

"I was going to kill you. I swear it," he began to explain as the sobs subsided. "I've been in the club having a right skin-full, working up the courage to come up here."

"But why Billy? I don't understand why," I genuinely enquired.

Billy fumbled with his eye to remove a contact lens, walked into the kitchen and dropped it into the bowl of a small spoon. He removed his other contact lens and turned to face me.

"Celia has thrown me out," he said despondently. "It wasn't her, it was her cow of a mother. Her and her dad. Always talking to her, whispering in her ear, turning her against me."

I motioned for him to join me back in the lounge as he told me how he'd found his belongings on the doorstep, and a 'Dear John' note pinned to the door.

He was angry, the type of fury that only rejection could spawn. He'd thought of different scenarios but settled on one: to kill me, strangle Celia, snap his baby's neck and take a hammer to her parents' heads. *Oh, you're in deep here, Walker* I thought to myself. I hadn't signed up for this.

Cucumber sandwiches and garden parties, visiting elderly parishioners and chatting over a slice of cake – yes. Dealing with someone intent on murder – no. I had in no way been prepared for this. Whether he meant it or not, whether he would have gone on and carried out his killing spree if he'd got the better of me, I couldn't say. But my splintered door frame told a tale of determined anger.

As we spoke, I steered the conversation to his need for God. I explained where I was heading that night and asked if he'd like to come. Desperate times sometimes call for desperate measures, and he acquiesced.

"Sure, why not. What else is there to do now?" he said.

We were late to the venue after a 50-minute drive from the village. As we took our seats at the back, worship was already in full swing. A preacher stood up and spoke of man's need for God, of how only God could make sense of life, how only God could make you feel loved as you were meant to be, how he could forgive you and give you a new life and fresh hope.

Billy was hanging on his every word. The preacher made an altar call, a chance for those who were ready to come forward and give their lives to Jesus. Billy was squirming in his seat. He seemed ready to go forward but was struggling to make the move.

"Do you want to go forward?" I whispered.

"Yes," was his reply, "But I aren't doing it here. If I'm going to do it, it'll be at Church House with you."

I couldn't believe what was happening. If Billy decided to follow God, the news would spread like wildfire through the estate; it would light the blue touch paper and my ministry would take off. If God could reach him, he could reach anyone! I'd be beating off the queue of converts with a King James Bible! We slipped out and drove in silence back towards Bluebell Common. The atmosphere in the car was electric, the anticipation was building. I didn't dare speak in case it distracted him from his decision. As we neared the estate, Billy said, "Pull over. I'm going to stay at my mate's."

"But what about the prayer? You said you wanted to give your life to Jesus," I stammered, confused.

"I'm not that easy," he replied, as he opened the door and disappeared into the dark of the night, leaving me deflated.

All those fantasies of a streetfighter converted to Christianity were done with. He had been so close, but the moment had gone, and with it the chance to make a huge impact on the life of the estate.

That wasn't to be the last I saw of Billy. Our paths were to cross several times, but our meetings were never as dramatic again. I would often ponder over what happened that night. Could I have done things differently? Perhaps I should have pushed him to answer the altar call; who knows what would've happened if he'd gone forward that night?

Within a year Billy found himself as a resident of Her Majesty's Prison Hull, after a bungled attempted armed robbery of a sub post office. He'd brandished a toy gun wrapped in a carrier bag at the cashier.

"Give me all the money or I'll blow your fucking head off," he shouted.

"Piss off!" came the reply. The plastic bag was so thin that she could see the gun was a toy.

He fled empty handed and was picked up by a police patrol following a brief manhunt.

I am looking at a letter he wrote to me on prison stationery on 26 April 1990, in which he wrote, "I am going to chapel tomorrow. That's a laugh coming from me, I am just goin' cos it's something to do on a Sunday morning. You never know Seth I might even end up turning Christian if this shithole starts getting to me. But I doubt that it will."

I later found out that he didn't make it to chapel. Instead, he ended up serving a month in the punishment block. He'd been given a new cell mate. He welcomed him, shared his tobacco with him and a friendship had started to form. That was until the grapevine started buzzing with some fresh news. A fellow prisoner told Billy that his new pad mate was a nonce, a child sex offender, and it was Billy's job to make him pay. It was an SOS job, smash on sight. Billy had to boot up and obey the law of this concrete and steel jungle, so he beat him badly enough to earn the respect of his peers and a full month in the block.

When my time at Bluebell Common drew to a close, I thought that Billy would no longer be part of my life. I'd been given an extended break to recover from such an intense experience. During my final Episcopal review, the bishop recognised that my ministry had exacted a personal, emotional and psychological toll.

"I am concerned that he has not been taking adequate time off recently." This was an understatement. I received the following transcript of a letter written to the bishop by one of my Bluebell Common parishioners, in which she wrote words which still make me break down and cry. I'm now far removed from the life of the church and find it hard to identify with the person she's writing about: "The amount of service he puts himself forward for is truly amazing. Sleepless nights and busy days are all part of his work and he never moans. He is open and honest and discusses many of the things he would want to accomplish here, when others are ready to give up. He has earned the respect of the village and love of us all."

I'd already moved into the curate's house in my new parish but not yet started my new ministry when I received a phone call that reminded me the past is never far away. For the last six months of my time at Bluebell Common, I'd been looking after the larger parish church, my boss having moved on to bigger and better things in a neighbouring diocese. The call was from James's replacement.

"Seth, do you remember Mike and Beth?" he asked.

My mind went back to the night I'd helped Beth by removing all the knives from the house and facing Mike off when he'd spoken about killing his family.

"Yes I do, she's a lovely person and a big part of the church at Bluebell Common," was my reply.

"Well, I'm afraid they're having some trouble with someone."

"No, that's awful. They could do without any more trouble; that's the last thing that family needs," I responded.

"Yes, I agree. Beth tells me that Billy and Mike have had an argument," he began to explain.

I found this puzzling: Billy – now out of prison – and Mike moved in different circles, and to my knowledge had nothing to do with each other. If there had been an argument, then something had gone badly wrong.

"Beth says that Billy has threatened Mike with a handgun and says that he's going to shoot him," he explained.

I took this with a pinch of salt. If Billy wanted to shoot Mike, why hadn't he done it then and there when he had a gun with him? Knowing Mike's propensity for fantasy, and knowing that firearms were hard to come by despite what the printed news media proclaimed, I doubted this had taken place. Billy had no access to guns; I was fairly convinced that was out of his league. To get your hands on a firearm required a considerable financial outlay, and Billy wasn't exactly flush the last time I saw him.

"Well, what you need to do is to go and see Billy," I offered. "I'd say to him, 'Look, I know that Mike has been a pain in the ass, and we all know what he's like, but for the sake of Beth and the kids, please could you lay off – and I'll tell Mike to back off.' That should be a way in. That's how I'd have handled it. If you go and see Billy, you'll probably find out that there's no gun, and Billy probably doesn't want to get involved in anything that will send him back to prison anyway. Billy has been keeping his nose clean to keep out."

"Ah, yes." He paused and sounded as if he was trying to come to a decision. "I wonder if you'd be prepared to come back and talk with Billy? After all, you've built a relationship with him."

That was the moment I realised all the good the work I'd done at Bluebell Common probably wouldn't continue; that perhaps the same level of day-to-day, close-up and personal ministry would no longer take place. "I'm sorry," I replied. "But the bishop has been quite firm with me; I have to make the break."

But I am glad that I met Billy and shared those occasionally terrifying experiences with him. I only hope that what little I had to offer eased his inner turmoil and, perhaps, stopped his violent plan in its tracks and saved a family from tragedy.

Chapter 16

MIRACLE AND ANTI-MIRACLE

I was a Bible-believing Christian, which meant I should believe the world was only 6,000 years old, evolution was the devil's work, the Grand Canyon was carved during Noah's flood, God didn't like you thinking about sex, and miracles happened, even in today's world.

When miraculous healings didn't happen, it was your fault because you didn't have enough faith or because you'd committed some awful sin. I knew my literal understanding of the scriptures would take a battering at theological college, but for me, there was no other way. My Old Testament lecturer asked me which textbook concordance I was using, When I said, "Cruden's", he replied "Ah, Cruden's for the crude in faith." I'm still in contact with him today and his summary wasn't far from the truth.

I may have been crude in faith, but to me God was either Lord of all or not Lord at all. I couldn't see how you could pick and choose which part of the Bible to believe in; it came as a complete package. If you picked at the loose threads of scripture, the whole thing would soon fall apart. No, it all had to be God's word, taken on faith, or it was a worthless collection of folktales.

Along with that came a belief that miracles, like the ones recorded in the Bible, did happen; more than that, those who followed God should have enough faith to take him at his word and expect them to happen today. And that's what I believed I could experience in my ministry.

I approached the conservatory which took up three quarters of Gloria's yard, noticing the small figure of three-year-old Sam napping in a push-along buggy. Gloria was a stalwart of the church: her large extended family was scattered throughout the village but didn't attend church. She had several sons in the village, all with the reputation of being skilled street fighters. She could leave her house unlocked, unoccupied, and with all her goods on display and no one would dare burgle her.

That might be doing her an injustice; Gloria would never falter in her good work or fail to help out anyone in genuine need. She had a deep seam of kindness, backed up with a strength of character that had withstood life's hardest tests. But that particular day she seemed sad.

She'd been telling me how ill Sam was: he wasn't sleeping at night, he dozed fitfully during the day, he refused to eat and didn't play with his brothers and sisters. I'd told her

I'd pray for him, and this seemed like an ideal chance. I gently knocked on Gloria's back door and stepped inside. I explained to her what I had in mind, and we snuck back outside so as not to wake Sam up. I placed my hands gently on his head and prayed in the name of Jesus that the Lord would heal him. In theory I believed in miracles; I'd seen little to back this up in practice. But it was my experience that people derived some benefit just from being prayed for, and that was enough for me.

I don't think I honestly expected that Sam would be healed, but something did occur. Over a cup of tea and a chocolate biscuit, Gloria explained to me that the doctor had diagnosed something called pernicious anaemia. I'd never heard of it before, and made a mental note to ask my dad, who'd been a pharmacist for 30 years. I left Gloria's house and thought no more about it until I saw her again at mid-week Bible study.

"Great news Seth," she gushed. "Sam's better!"

"What do you mean, better?" I replied, surprised.

"Well, after you prayed with him, our Lisa pushed him home in the buggy, but he was still asleep. He slept all afternoon, woke up and said he wanted some tea. He never usually eats, he just grazes and doesn't have much of an appetite. But he ate all his tea, and pudding, and then said he was tired and went to bed. He slept all night, got up, had breakfast and went out to play and he's been alright since. It's a miracle!" she explained.

At first glance it did indeed seem as if something out of the ordinary had taken place, if you presented the facts in a certain way. We prayed for him, and he was healed. He'd slept at night and eaten, which he hadn't been doing, and he'd found the energy to play with his brothers and sisters, which he seemed to have lost.

I'd been brought up to believe in the God of miracles, and here was some small evidence that suggested he was still alive and in the business of performing mighty miraculous acts.

However, before I file this under the category of divine intervention, another explanation may be worth pursuing. Pernicious anaemia, while fairly rare, is not that unusual in the world of medicine. Sam's mum had taken him to the doctor, where He'd been diagnosed and treated with vitamin B12. My prayer coincided with this medical intervention; while a miracle did indeed occur, it was more likely a miracle of modern medical science.

I used to tell this story when I was a Christian, sometimes in a sermon, and use it as proof of a miraculous God. Looking back now with the eyes of the sceptic, I'm a little bit ashamed that I claimed the power of science as some supernatural act of healing.

I visited Gloria over 20 years later for a catch up, and Sam, now a grown man, was also there. His wasn't a courtesy visit to his grandmother though; he was hiding from drug dealers who he owed money to. They'd threatened him with a beating and he was frightened. Gloria implored me to speak to him, telling him to listen to what I had to say, but my words were feeble and had no impact. Sam was in trouble, and it would take a real miracle to turn his life around.

We live in a world saturated by information: an information-rich but in some ways a knowledge-poor society. The world was a different place 30 years ago, and the God of the gaps had bigger gaps to inhabit. There seemed more room for the spiritual and the supernatural in our lives, which wasn't always a good thing. I had begun to study parapsychology, and this was starting to have an impact on my faith.

I developed a routine whereby I appeared to bend spoons with psychic energy; the more I practised, the better I got. I could use mind power to move an object in a 'sealed' container and could remotely view people's drawings whilst simultaneously stopping my heart from beating. Anyone can learn these tricks, but they were dramatic, and I used them to debunk belief in new-age, supposedly psychic phenomena.

I used my research to help a new colleague who was troubled by an encounter in Indonesia with a woman who described herself as a witch. She had apparently told him things about his life that only he could know. She had also told him there was a curse on him that would mean an early death. She could remove it for a sum of money, but as a poor student traveller about to return to the UK, he couldn't afford it and was now frightened. The fear was growing and beginning to cause sleepless nights and anxiety.

I'd spent little time with him and didn't know much about his background, but I knew how to 'cold read', a technique used by mediums to pick up on clues and cues from their clients to make their abilities sound miraculous. I don't doubt this had taken place in Indonesia, but perhaps if I could replicate it, I could help him see that it was little more than a confidence trick, designed to part him from his money.

So I began the cold reading. I told him that his father was a professional man with a well-paid job, clear from his accent and the fact he'd been to university, not the norm 30 years ago. I told him that when he was a child, his father was a remote figure, working hard to establish himself in his career and studying at night for further professional qualifications. It was a punt, but it was spot on.

Sometimes his father would be tired and irritable and appear distant and unapproachable. Because of this, he spent a lot of time with his mother, becoming more comfortable in the company of women than men. I also said that some people had questioned his sexuality because of this, but he had no doubts. He was amazed how much I knew about him.

I weaved in the usual "at times you are happy and outgoing, but sometimes withdraw into yourself. You've been misunderstood and sometimes are careful with what you share. Love hasn't always been straightforward with you and money is often an issue." These are what are known as 'Forer statements': they apply to the vast majority of us. He wanted to know how I knew so much about him, but I explained that I didn't, and neither did the Indonesian witch.

No curse had been placed on his life, and skepticism proved useful in bringing him some relief from the fear the fake witch had exploited to try to cheat money from him.

This could also be applied to Christian miracle workers, which presented me with a problem: the same lessons I was learning to debunk psychic frauds had started to make inroads into my own faith.

I'd come across the concept of the anti-miracle from a church leader, who'd spoken about how other preachers experienced powerful miracles while the opposite was true in his own ministry. He spoke about how uncomfortable he felt when he was invited to sit on the stage during an old-fashioned healing meeting. At that time there was a craze a craze for leg growing: he was embarrassed to take part in the proceedings, but also too embarrassed to refuse.

An overweight person with a thyroid problem was attempting to walk up the steep steps to the stage to receive their healing, when they missed a step, fell backwards several feet and broke a leg. An ambulance had to be called to take him to hospital to receive a genuine healing intervention; the church leader described this as an anti-miracle.

Another example was when he was leading a meeting, and a member of the congregation was convinced God had moved them to prophecy, and had given them a picture showing his intentions for London. When the speaker gave this person a microphone so they could share this divine message, they declared they saw God in the shape of an octopus, with his testicles spreading over every corner of London. I broke out into unstoppable laughter when I heard this humorous example of an anti-miracle. Little was I to know that I too would experience the power of the anti-miracle in my own ministry.

I had been called to a hospital in a nearby town to visit the mother of one of my new parish's most fervent church members. She was nearly 90 and seriously ill. After being in hospital for a number of days, the doctors were convinced the end was near.

Taking her age, her illness and the doctors' words into account, I'd decided that I would pray for her using the words of the song of Simeon, the Nunc Dimittis. Simeon was an elderly man who attended the temple each day in the hope of seeing the promised messiah; the Holy Spirit had told him that he would live to see him and he held on for this momentous occasion. When Jesus entered the temple, Simon declared, " Lord, now lettest thou thy servant depart in peace." As I approached the bedside, children and grandchildren looked on with concern as she laboured over every breath. She was in a side room, not an open ward, which gave us some privacy. I prayed with the family that God would work to produce the best outcome, that they might receive comfort in the midst of their mourning and remember their loved one with peace.

I asked for some time alone with the lady. I held her hand as her shallow, rapid breathing rasped. I read the words of the Nunc Dimittis and said, "You've done so well, it's now time for you to let go, to have a rest and be at peace with your family around you, it's time to let go." I prayed that God would grant her the rest she deserved and receive her into his eternal kingdom, ending her suffering once and for all. I felt moved by my own prayers and saddened to be present during the last moments of this person's life. I stood up and invited the family back in, thinking I shouldn't intrude on what were sure to be private, personal moments. I left the hospital, climbed into my car and started to make a few notes for the funeral. I carried on with the rest of the business of the day and returned home for tea.

As I brewed a fresh pot of coffee I could see the answerphone light flashing. *No rest for the righteous*, I thought, as I played the message:

"Whatever you said to Mum when you were on your own with her clearly worked. 20 minutes after you left, she sat bolt upright and asked for bread and jam. It's a miracle."

MIRACLE AND ANTI-MIRACLE

I never explained to the family the exact nature of my prayers: I didn't want to seem foolish, because the opposite of what I had prayed for had occurred. Whilst slightly amusing, this was another incident that led me to question the power of prayer and the existence of another realm, a spiritual realm which could make a visible, tangible and detectable impact on our lives.

These two incidents seemed to suggest to me that prayer definitely works, as long as it's in line with what's going to happen anyway.

Chapter 17

ALL CHANGE

As my time at Bluebell Common drew to a close, the bishop had made a decision concerning my future. He'd seen enough to be sure that the right move would be to ordain me. I would finally gain the prized dog collar which I'd craved over the past few years! Gone would be the lengthy explanation to receptionists, policemen or nurses, of who I was and why I was there; one look at my dog collar would open previously closed doors.

Saying goodbye to Bluebell Common and its mother parish of Larkwood was tough. I'd invested a lot in the village and was to learn the hard way that when you leave, you have to let go and allow the work to move on in a different direction, steered by others.

I knew there'd be a gap before my post would be filled. I had met my successor: he was a family man, and as such, he didn't feel that he could live in the village. This troubled me; I didn't want the people of Bluebell Common to feel that the church didn't accept them for who they were. At that stage, I suppose that my theology had already started to shift from an emphasis on the centrality of what Jesus did in dying on the cross towards the important symbolism of his coming into the world and taking on human form. There's something powerful in being prepared to immerse yourself in the world of those you are trying to serve.

I thought that I'd managed to capture some of that powerful message and convey it to the village just by living there alongside them. On my last day, I was talking to Billy and Darren, a small-time drug dealer and ex-football hooligan.

"Thanks for looking out for me, it's appreciated," I said. "I haven't had a window broken or been burgled. So thanks for putting the word out."

I'd assumed that I was under their protection. I'd helped them both out and thought they had my back. This assumption wasn't without basis: They'd put the frighteners on someone called Dave who they believed had hurt me. In fact, Dave was actually a friend then, and still is today. He's a good six foot two and outweighs me by a wide margin. He'd come to stay the night and see what I was doing. After a couple of convivial beers, he punched me playfully on the arm.

"Are you still hard, Seth?" he said, as another blow landed. This took me back 10 years when we would play-fight. I punched him back with a bit too much force.

"I don't know," I replied. "You tell me."

Dave didn't use words to reply, but fists. I slipped what I could, turning my head to take the sting of a blow that connected, I stepped inside his long reach to pummel his ribs. Down he went. This wasn't a rare occurrence back in the day, when play-fighting sometimes overstepped the mark, but now we were grown men and I was a church minister. He got up but wasn't happy and came at me again; this was getting a bit serious. I targeted his ribs again and dropped him a second time.

"Mate, this is daft," I said. "I'm stepping out for some fresh air." As I leant against the wall breathing heavily, with one of my knuckles bleeding, Billy walked past.

"What's up, Seth?" he asked. "Been in a rumble?"

"Aye, I have," I replied. "There's a big lad in my house; I've just put him down." Time to earn some kudos.

"Do you want us to sort him out?" Billy offered.

An idea popped into my head. I knew it was probably wrong, but the adrenaline was still flowing. Dave had wanted to come and see my world – well, he could get a close-up view.

"No, there's no need for that. I don't need anyone to fight my battles," I said. "But why don't you go in and put the frighteners on him. Don't touch him though, he's supposed to be a mate!" I called, as Billy ran over the road.

A minute later he was back with Darren.

"Don't touch him!" I said, as they went into my house. I only have Dave's account of what happened; it's a story he still enjoys telling today. He was sat down getting his breath back when two tattooed street fighters entered the room and stood over him with an air gun. They stared at him for a while, cocked the gun, pointed it at him and fired it, unloaded. Their only words to him were: "You fuck with Seth and you fuck with us."

It's safe to say that Dave had a greater understanding of my workplace after that incident.

That was why I thought I was under their protection and why I was thanking them before I left Bluebell Common for good.

"No, Seth," Darren replied. "We haven't put the word out. People knew if they messed with you, you'd kick the shit out of them."

I was simultaneously proud and upset at that remark. These mixed emotions were to form a suitable epitaph for my time at Bluebell Common. I'd been blissfully ignorant and misunderstood the situation; I was also misunderstood by others.

Over the years I've learned to worry less about what people think about me and what I say and do; they probably don't understand my reasons or appreciate that they come from a place of love and care.

Sometimes, after sampling a fine malt whisky of an evening, my thoughts turn back to those days, and even now I question my motives for some of my actions, but the difference between then and now is I'm at peace and glad I tried to help.

The next step was for me to take the cloth, to become a member of the clergy. I wasn't asked to attend the usual selection weekend, involving a lengthy process which may, if you are not sifted out like chaff, culminate in ordination. In the bishop's eyes, I had already undergone my three years of training at theological college, so it'dbe a waste of time and resources to send me back there. He was also sure of the authenticity of my calling.

Although I was to avoid the selection process, I still had many interviews with the Diocesan Director of Ordinands. These were made all the more pleasant because he was a great man and we had mutual friends.

I sometimes wonder whether the bishop had been influenced by his housekeeper. She was a formidable lady and a family friend. It was at my mother's recommendation that she'd applied for the post of residential housekeeper to the bishop. She got the job, and as I was good friends with her son, I'm sure she whispered in the bishop's ear on more than one occasion.

Her son and I used to go fell running, on the South Pennine moors. On Tuesday evenings we would drive out to a remote valley, run over Bell House Moor, touch the monument on Stoodley Pike and begin the descent, splashing through streams and ploughing through bogs.

We would return to Bishop's Croft, shower, change, and head down to the local pub to slake our thirst. The bishop stopped me on one of these evenings.

"Seth, I want you to use my shower tonight and not the guest room. I've got the Archbishop of Canterbury staying, and I do not want you giving his wife a shock."

The bishop was wise, funny and at times gregarious, but he did not suffer fools gladly. It was a blow to the diocese when he retired.

My journey to the ordained ministry had begun over six years previously, when I enrolled at theological college. I hadn't entered this small religious learning community through the same route as my fellow students. Everyone else had been through a selection journey, with most candidates falling by the wayside. Many feel the call, but few are chosen. The route usually begins with a sense of calling, of growing service in your local parish. A recognition of that calling from your own minister and worshipping community may lead to your name being passed to the Diocesan Director of Ordinands. There then may follow an in-depth process involving a number of interviews, exploring your faith, your family background, your journey towards ministry, and psychological probing; instructions to gain more life experience may then follow.

When the Diocesan Director of Ordinands is as sure of your sense of calling as you are, you begin the formal process of selection. Your suitability for ministry is tested further at residential retreats. You may be accepted as an ordinand and begin your residential theological studies for up to three years, with the prize of a degree in Theology to treasure as a result. If you pass the degree and successfully complete your placements in local churches, and if the college has no misgivings, you may then begin to look for a training parish that takes inexperienced, wet-behind-the-ears ordinands. You'd serve one year as a deacon there before your priestly ordination. You'd be moulded into a pastor, someone with the service of their community at the heart of all they do.

Not me though. I arrived as a private student. A visiting preacher had laid his hands on my head and prophesied over me several years previously. He proclaimed that God had a plan for my life; he'd given me a pastor's heart and one day I'd be in a position of leadership in the church.

I was becoming increasingly convinced this was the path I should tread. One of our church leaders was, too. He was concerned that a wave of miracle teaching, of seeking out religious experiences, had started to take precedence over the authority of the Bible. He thought that if this continued, then what we experience, how we were feeling, would start to dictate the direction of the church rather than the teachings of scripture. He pulled a small group of young people together and we started to study the Bible. He shared his theology with me over long runs out towards the moors. He was a big, quiet, strong and wise man. His intervention led to me exploring the possibility of gaining a degree in Theology to build the foundation of knowledge I'd need if I was to serve God and be true to my growing calling.

Tragically I wasn't to see him again for another 19 years, until a chance meeting in a hospital lift, when a short, elderly man tugged at my sleeve.

"Hey up Seth, how's tricks?"

The voice was familiar, as was the face, but his body had been ravaged by a progressive disease of the nervous system; it was clearly in its advanced stages: his body trembled and he was bent in on himself. It was a bittersweet meeting, but I try to remember him running over the hills or sparring with a man half his age; not as the old man in the lift.

The admissions tutor at the college wasn't sure about my application. I didn't want the full experience of an ordinand, but just a thorough theological grounding. An appointment was made and I was interviewed, thoroughly grilled in fact. There was no problem with my scriptural knowledge, but I had no linguistic skills, no understanding of New Testament Greek or Hebrew. I had a narrow and dogmatic faith, little experience of the rich pallet of Christian doctrine and no knowledge of church history or traditions. However, he saw something in me, and I received a letter offering me a place.

I threw myself into every aspect of college life. I took part in daily worship, then joined the rota to help lead services. I joined the college running team, competing in the London Universities and Colleges Athletics running fixtures. I also joined the rugby and football teams.

I wrote the college pantomime and end of year review along with three friends. I was placed in local churches and as my sense of mission, of calling, began to grow, I organised a youth mission accepting an increasing number of preaching engagements. This was enhanced by attending a communication course, run by one of the premier stage schools in the country. We were taught how to breathe, how to use our diaphragm to help project our voices and how to vary our tone and speed to hold an audience. This had a positive impact on my delivery and my preaching improved.

As my knowledge developed, I was asked to contribute book reviews to an evangelical periodical. Something was changing inside me; I was growing as a person and felt my faith was taking me in a different direction. The days were full of devotion, study, fun, sport, laughter and tears as I experienced the wear and tear of community life. Each summer I interned for an international evangelistic association, gaining experience well beyond my years.

Service was at the heart of our life. We had weekly duties and our own areas of responsibility, and I supplemented this by being voted onto the college council as my year representative. We had weekly kitchen duties, and once a fortnight an afternoon spent gardening with the maintenance team. 21 of us shared a lounge, kitchen and bathrooms and we learned to accept each other for who we were. Community living is not always easy, but the sense of family was palpable.

ALL CHANGE

In my final year of living in this religious community, I made an appointment with my own Diocesan Director of Ordinands, and my journey to ministry was clearly well established.

And now, four years on, whether influenced by the fat file on me, or by sources closer to home, the bishop's mind was made up and I was ordained into the diaconate (the office of a deacon). More than that, I was assigned to a training parish, to learn from an experienced priest. I was to serve a curacy under the guidance and authority of Father Paul, in a liberal Anglo-Catholic parish.

Theologically my new parish was diametrically opposed to the charismatic, non-conformist Christianity II'dbeen brought up in. It was also far removed – in fact, at the far end of the spectrum – from Bluebell Common.

I did have some measure of choice as to where I should serve my curacy, as did my prospective parish. Despite the theological mismatch, we seemed a good fit.

I was aware that although I had considerable experience for one so young, I wanted to see what this branch of the church was all about; to immerse myself in this previously alien doctrine, to worship in a different manner and hopefully learn a new way to minister.

After ordination, you serve a year as deacon, which roughly translates as 'servant': you serve God's people, but also the parish priest. You're still not permitted to administer certain sacraments; the idea being that after in-depth study at theological college, you gain practical experience at the coalface of ministry. You get the chance to ground that theory in the day-to-day ministry of parish life.

That year also serves as a winnowing process: you'll soon discover if you're not right for service. It's not a given that you become a priest and enter the college of presbyters 12 months later.

Having been ordained in a way that bucked convention, the bishop was concerned that I should follow the time-honoured pathway to my priestly ordination, so I engaged in a full programme of what was known as 'potty training'. This was the amusing title given to our post-ordination training, and allowed us to gain useful insight into what it means to be an effective priest.

I first met Charles during some of these sessions. He was a striking character who looked more like a rock musician than an ordained minister. He had long, blond hair which fell towards his shoulders. He never wore clerical garb; his outfit was unconventional, gothic even, and he radiated a charisma that few possessed. I was sure I'd met him before.

Charles was the figurehead of a new church movement, a movement that had gained momentum and seen several hundred young people attending a new style of worship. Charles's ordination was part of a strategy to ensure that the church continued to be relevant to the younger generation.

ALL CHANGE

The movement was based around a youth service, held initially within a large church in the centre of the recession-hit town. The elements of worship were drawn from an eclectic bunch of influences, including the dance music scene which had blossomed in the late 1980s and 1990s, the use of visual media and a theology based on God's presence in creation.

I well remember the pageantry surrounding Charles during the preparation for our priestly ordination. There was talk of acolytes who served him; whether this was true or not I don't know, but certainly more people attended to him than the whole of the rest of the ordinands put together. It was strange to see people dressing him, making sure that none of his priestly apparel was out of place.

I remembered this scene several years later when this movement imploded. Rumours of inappropriate behaviour became solid accusations. A scandal unfolded that would blight the lives of hundreds of people in that town; it reached the national news, leading to much corporate soul-searching over how this could ever have happened. One of our family friends was caught up in the midst of this and suffered deeply as a result.

But all that was way off in the future. I was to submerge myself in the life of parish ministry and experience a different way of serving the church.

Father Paul's church differed from Bluebell Common in that all the barriers between church and community were removed, leaving the parishioners feeling there was no reason for them not to be part of the life of the church. You didn't have to attend baptism classes before your child could be christened. There were no marriage preparation courses, no Bible study groups, no need to attend an enquiry group. The church was seen as being an integral part of the community, as accessible as going to the pub for a pint, getting on a bus, or going to do your weekly shopping.

At Bluebell Common however, if you wanted to be part of the church, you had to decide to follow Jesus. This would involve repentance and bowing the head to Jesus before entering into the life of the church. You'd have to attend Bible study groups, and, if you were new in the faith, scripture lessons.

In my new parish, St Paul's, everyone who had been baptised, usually when infants, was considered to be a legitimate member of the church. The barriers were removed, and all were welcome. One of the early Christian theologians said that what Jesus didn't take on, he didn't heal, meaning that when he took on full humanity, he restored us as God's children. This theology was being worked out in practice here. Jesus had come into the world as one of us, and had opened the door of faith to us all.

I found it refreshing, but could not reconcile it to over two decades of the evangelical, charismatic theology I'd experienced and latterly taught. My previous incarnation of Christianity emphasised our sinfulness and the subsequent need for forgiveness: original sin had stained our souls and only the blood of Jesus could wash that taint away. Yes, Jesus had come into the world; yes, he had died on the cross that our sins might be forgiven; but we weren't part of the church until we'd turned our backs on our previous lives, begged forgiveness and pledged allegiance to him. Sin had created a barrier between us and God; it was up to us to take up the offer of redemption, to be saved.

In Father Paul's parish, Jesus's redemption was enough. He'd taken away the legacy of sin and the way to God was open to all; there was no need for you to adopt sackcloth and ashes. I relished this concept, of the church being part of one's everyday life.

This approach opened many doors to me. I found myself doing chaplaincy work in an ambulance station, post Hillsborough, hearing horrific tales of what was experienced on that day; the lasting imprint on those who provided first aid and emergency treatment was plain to see.

I served as a governor at two local schools, becoming involved in the education of our parish children in a way that never happened during my time at Bluebell Common. I taught lessons, led assemblies and started a counselling service during my time there, working with staff as well as pupils, who were all struggling with the massive upheaval to the education system as local management of schools was implemented.

We worked alongside our local MPs to address social inequalities, and these MPs also became part of the life of our parish. I remember an MP who went on to become a senior government figure turning up to a community meeting to discuss a strategy for reclaiming the streets. He had his personal assistant with him and was carrying a leather satchel full of papers concerning those people he knew would be at the meeting. People were asking questions that they'd previously broached at a constituency surgery, and he would have an answer for them somewhere in that leather bag.

The theology seemed to match the politics: no divide, no them and us, no barriers. We were in it together, and we were going to do our best to make a difference and build a better society.

Gone was the sense of me battling against spiritual principalities and powers, and in its place was a wider calling, a calling for a practical outworking of the gospel, to meet social needs. Lord Shaftesbury, the Victorian reformer, had once said that "But when people say we should think more of the soul and less of the body, my answer is, that the same God who made the soul made the body also." I could see this being put into practice in this parish.

However, although I'd made a break with the past, it wasn't long before I found myself dealing with an all-too-familiar incident.

Chapter 18

WRESTLING WITH DEMONS

One Thursday night saw a rare occasion for St Paul's: one of only three evening services we celebrated in a year. Father Paul was on leave, so it fell to me to conduct the simple said Communion for the Mothers' Union. With 15 minutes to go, I left the curate's house wearing my dog collar and black cassock, and began the short walk to the church.

I got as far as two houses away when Bill, a neighbour in his 50s, came running out of his garden and stopped me. He was red faced and clearly upset, but I registered something else about him. His eyes were wide, like a deer caught in headlights. He was clearly terrified. He was experiencing a monster shot of adrenaline: fight or flight. It looked as if he was intent on flight.

"Father Seth. You've got to help me. My wife's possessed and I don't know what to do!"

Sweet baby Jesus. I stood open-mouthed. What? I was trying to process what I'd just been told. Panic can be contagious – the terror that was clearly gripping Bill started to reach out to me. My previous encounters with Bill made it even more difficult to make sense of; I'd only ever seen him calm, tending to his front garden. Exchanges of pleasantries over the fence, a mild chide from me that you can clean your car at other times than Sunday mornings, was the extent of our contact. At each encounter he appeared to be a calm, even-tempered Yorkshireman. Not tonight though. Anxiety, fear and a sense of urgency replaced stoicism.

As a priest it's important to be able to detach yourself from a situation, to step outside the bubble and not be a part of the drama of the moment. To minister effectively, you have to be walking on the water, like Jesus, not submerged in a sea of grief, anger, hate or, in this case, fear.

Easier said than done.

Bill grabbed my arms tightly and pulled me towards his house. "Come on!"

I took a step forward to avoid being pulled over. His insistence and the lack of time to make sense of his words, appearance and actions left me no space for detachment. I gaped at him and started to stutter. "What?" I was being pulled down into the stormy water.

A second "what" became "Wait!" as I managed to pull away. "Take a breath Bill. Say it again." This gave me a chance to regain my composure.

"It's Joan. She's got the devil in her. You've got to help us."

Great. In a few minutes I was supposed to begin Holy Communion in the church. Bill was desperate, insistent. But I couldn't abandon one of only three evening services we held in a year.

Father Paul was a liberal Anglo-Catholic; he would've seen this as a case of mental illness, best dealt with by a doctor. Demons belonged to a pre-enlightened age of ignorance and superstition, but not for Bill: this was happening now, in the age of the microchip.

"Bill. I will help. But I can't come now."

His face fell.

"One hour. I promise. Hold it together for one hour. I will be back."

I left a disconsolate man as I hurried to church. I may have set the world Holy Communion speed record that night.

After five minutes spent chatting with the ladies of the Mothers' Union, I returned to the vestry. Picking up a crucifix and a copy of the night prayers service booklet, I headed back down the road with my robes still on.

I didn't have time to contact the diocesan exorcist; I didn't even know who he was. His predecessor's one and only exorcism concluded with the supposed demons refusing to leave their host, so he'd be no help.

What do I do? I thought. A crisis was happening in a normal-looking house to a normal-looking family.

I knew I'd have to go in alone, with no back-up, no prayer team, no psychological profile, no chain of authority above me. I felt exposed and worried that I'd be out of my depth. What if I made a huge mistake and it all went south? The words my father used in answer to those who sat back and offered criticism with the luxury of 20/20 hindsight came to my mind: "I prefer the way I did it to the way you didn't."

At least I should go in and offer some support to Bill, shouldn't I?

It's hard to describe the fear, the dread, that took my self-confidence from me. You try to be rational and convince yourself that demons are part of a long-dead folklore, with no place in the modern world. But fear works at a different level to reason. It taps into a primordial part of our being. The amygdala, an almond-sized fear-primed region of our brain located deep within the temporal lobes shrinks our thoughts to the instant, seeing fear and acting to survive its cause. No time for great inner discourses or reasoned thought; it heightens our perception and focuses on the instant, making us act on instinct.

In my case, as an educated graduate, schooled in philosophy, I knew that talk of demons sounded ridiculous, but my amygdala was wrestling for control with the rational part of me. Memories of my childhood night terrors shot into my mind like fiery arrows, confusing me and clouding my judgement.

I shook my head and asked God to help me, to be with me and to keep me safe. I knocked on the door and waited for just a few seconds. It was opened by a calmer Bill.

"Come in Father, come in." He beckoned me into the kitchen.

"How is she?" I asked.

"Calmer," He replied, troubled. "But she still isn't right."

"Can she hear us in here?"

I asked this for a reason. I needed to get my head round what had been going on and find out if I was really needed there; perhaps a doctor or a community psychiatric nurse would be better suited to her need.

"No, but she knows it's you that's calling around. She's been sat there using her voices saying you're too scared to show up."

"Voices?" I asked incredulously.

"Aye. She talks in different voices."

I was soon to discover that she used three different 'voices': her own, a deep male voice and the sugary pleading of a little girl.

"And that's not all. She hits me." He hung his head in shame and I was struck with pity for this poor, beleaguered man. "She's a damn sight stronger than me. I can't stop her. It's not right by my way of thinking."

My eyebrows rose in disbelief as I took in Bill's stocky frame. She must be some size, I thought.

"Bill, I'm going to go in. Do you mind if I leave these here?" I held up the service book and crucifix, not wanting to prompt an immediate response when I entered the room.

"Oh, alright, you know what you're about." Bill expressed a faith in me I didn't feel myself.

I opened the lounge door and looked in. I saw nothing out of the ordinary. It was a modestly appointed, clean and largely tidy room, carpeted, attractively decorated and maintained with pride. There was a television and video cassette recorder in front of the window, facing a grey fabric sofa. On the sofa sat Joan.

I stopped, slightly puzzled, because I had expected to see a large-framed woman, powerfully built, capable of attacking her stocky husband and knocking him to the floor. Instead I could see a petite, thin lady in her early 50s, probably no more than five feet in height. I couldn't see her face clearly as she'd turned her head to the left and down towards her chest. Her brown and grey hair hung over the right side of her face, all but obscuring it. A glint of reflected light through her hair indicated she was watching me closely.

"Hi Joan," I greeted, as I tried to establish eye contact.

There was no sense of fear, no icy atmosphere and no strange smells to indicate anything supernatural was taking place. Just this small woman contorted in on herself with her arms wrapped around her, looking at me awkwardly through one eye like an animal caught in a trap.

"I hope you don't mind?" I asked, as I walked towards the VCR. I fumbled for the eject button and pressed it. This seemingly bizarre action was standard operating procedure when called in to help people who claimed to be struggling with dark forces. If the video that ejected was *The Exorcist*, *The Amityville Horror* or something similar, then a good talking-to over a cup of tea and a quick prayer of blessing usually settled things down. All that popped up from the top of the VCR was a blank cassette that had been used to record a soap opera. I stood up and turned towards the sofa.

"I know your father!" A deep growling voice spat at me from just a foot away. I believe that if I hadn't turned round at that point, I would've been pushed into the VCR unit. Joan had risen quickly and silently from the sofa and was now stood facing me.

"I know your father!" she repeated with venom. "I've been watching him for years."

To say I was startled would be an understatement; I was frightened. It was important for me to remain detached and avoid being sucked into the emotional storm that was about to break.

"Oh, Joan, in that case, you'll know his name," I replied, trying to sound more confident than I felt. "Why don't you tell me his name Joan?"

She emitted a low guttural growl, feral in nature.

In those days I believed in a demonic aspect to life; it was reasonable to think that powers and dominions existed with the purpose of defying God, defiling those that would seek to follow him. So I had to be sure that what I was dealing with there and then was indeed demonic in origin, rather than someone deliberately trying to fool me, or, indeed, someone who was mentally ill.

Bill had followed me into the room and had moved towards Joan as she rose from the sofa. This was fortunate, because as she growled, she sprang at me. Her hands reached up for the collar of the white surplice I was still wearing over my black cassock. She pulled with what felt like unnatural strength and I fell forward. As I stumbled, Bill lunged forward and grabbed her hands in a desperate attempt to loosen her grip as I was being forced to my knees. I reached up and tried to prise her fingers from my collar. Between us, Bill and I managed to break her grip and move her to the sofa.

As I stepped back, breathing heavily, I looked at her again as she twisted on the sofa, bending her head down to the left and into her chest. I took stock of the situation. I am five foot ten inches and, in those days, weighed eleven and a half stone, yet I had been taken to the ground by a seven-stone, 50-year-old lady. It took the combined strength of two grown men to break her iron grip. This unnatural force could be the sign of a demon, possibly the first *authentic* sign encountered so far this evening.

"That wasn't very nice was it?" she asked, in a high and childish voice. "Hitting a girl."

This twisting of the truth was a second sign that the prince of lies, the deceiver, might be at work.

"You're not going to hurt me again, are you?"

I was being spoken to by what sounded like a seven or eight-year-old girl. I was beginning to lose control and I couldn't make sense of what I was experiencing. I was out of my depth in deep, dark waters; I needed some help.

"Hold on to her, Bill," I called. "Watch her!"

My voice was sharp and high with emotion. I headed into the kitchen, picked up my crucifix and service book, straightened my robes and mouthed a quick, silent prayer before stepping back into the room. I was caught up in the drama of the moment, and yet I had my doubts.

As I entered the room she started to whimper, followed by a pathetic, childish sobbing.

"Joan, I'm just going to say a few prayers." I began to intone from the service of night prayer, starting with a short reading from St Peter's First Epistle: "Brethren, be sober, be watchful; because your enemy the devil, as a roaring lion, walks about, seeking for whom he may devour: resist him, steadfast in the faith."

No reaction.

I raised the crucifix while Bill relaxed his grip and bowed his head. I read on,

"From all evil dreams defend our vision, from night terrors and imaginations. Trample under our feet, our ghastly adversary, that contamination we may not experience."

At this she was on her feet, growling. "I know your father and I know you," she said and lunged at me, knocking the crucifix out of my hand.

I started to falter; was this genuine? Had the crucifix, the symbol of Jesus's triumph, caused this reaction? Was this a third sign?

"In the name of Jesus Christ I take authority over you. By the power of the blood of Christ I bind you and command you to leave this woman!"

No reaction... or was there? She'd frozen as if rooted to the spot.

"Joan. Joan. Can you hear me?" I asked softly.

She shook her head as if to clear her thoughts. "Hello. What are you doing here?" She seemed genuinely puzzled.

"I've just come for a cup of tea and a chat," I said, as calmly as I could manage. "Bill, put the kettle on, will you?"

I led Joan to the sofa and we sat down. Here was the real Joan, not twisted, tainted or consumed with anger.

There was a palpable sense of relief in the room. A collective sigh. As we sat down, my guard started to slip.

"Joan, you were saying?" I asked, as naturally and calmly as I could.

"I... I..." Joan stuttered, clearly puzzled as she tried to answer. "You know, I was saying... Did I say something? It's the strangest thing, I don't remember what I was saying."

She seemed genuinely to have no recollection of what had taken place since I entered the room. This lack of memory during similar episodes is taken by some as a further sign of authentic demonic activity.

I wasn't completely convinced. I would have expected some sense of the unnatural about the circumstance and situation. It is hard to explain, but I had no 'feeling' of an alien presence. Yes, there had been a display of strength, yes there was some claim of knowledge of me, but nothing anyone couldn't guess. I suspected it could all be explained using science, common sense and a knowledge of psychology.

I could hear the clatter of teacups as the door opened and Bill walked in carrying a tray, – not the best china, but everyday mugs: a small detail, but I'm so used to people trying to impress the curate with their best china and some fancy biscuits.

As Bill turned to me with the tray, indicating which mug was mine, Joan rose to her feet and attempted to grab it. Bill, seemingly having anticipated this, stepped back, turned on his heels and walked towards the kitchen to set the tray down. It was almost as if he had been prepared for this eventuality. This and the use of every-day expendable mugs set me thinking. I'm not sure I would've been able to react that fast. This was either an occurrence that was all too regular in this household, or there was another explanation.

I've never been involved in an occult event where I could be 100 per cent sure that demonic activity was taking place. We are conditioned by the media, the thrill of horror films and popular literature to know what to expect when a person is under diabolic influence. This occasion felt as if we were doing a dance. There was a rhythm, flow, and interchange between the dancers, all seeming to know the steps they needed and when they needed to take them. And there, that night, we all knew our steps.

What was I dealing with here? I'd no time to dwell on that question, as Joan turned her attention to me. I was at a disadvantage, seated and dressed in shoulder-to-floor-length robes, having hurried from the service. She tried to grab my hair: big mistake; I'm now completely bald on top and in those days had very little thatch on my roof. The attempt ended in a comedic slap on my head, which added to the ridiculousness of the situation.

Before she could launch a further attack, Bill wrapped his arms around her from behind, lifted her off her feet and walked her backwards.

I stood up and, in my most convincingly authoritative voice, declared, "In the name of Jesus Christ, king of kings and lord of lords, I command you to leave this woman now. I bind you in the name of Jesus!"

Each mention of Jesus had no noticeable effect; if there was truly a demonic entity present, the name of Jesus should surely have provoked a response. I was unsure what was happening here and didn't know what to do next.

I reached for my service booklet and began to read again: "Visit, we implore thee, O Lord, this dwelling, and thrust from it all the traps of our foes; let thy sacred cherubs reside here to keep us in peace; Amen."

Joan had slumped in Bill's arms and he walked her over to the sofa and set her down. It was an inelegant, clumsy manoeuvre which seemed to shake her awake again.

"Hello Father," she said as if nothing had happened. "What are you doing here?"

This was sinking into farce. I suspected we were play-acting. I'd been invited to take part in a badly scripted Hollywood B movie and was playing my part well. I don't mean that Joan and Bill were deliberately setting out to fool me, or themselves. We all have personas that we present to the world; I'm not the same person at work as I am when I'm romping at home with my children. I don't talk to my stepmother in the same way I speak to my wife. Personas. We all use them to good effect as we manoeuvre through different social situations. That night I believed we were all playing our part in what would be expected to happen during a clash with the demonic.

My doubts increased at the lack of response to Jesus's name. Joan would sometimes respond, sometimes not. I needed a break to gather my thoughts and I needed some help.

I had no doubt that if I carried on, the situation would develop into a dramatic 'final scene'. I was worried about my safety, Joan's sanity and the family's crockery.

"I was just leaving, Joan," I replied, as calmly as I could. "It's been lovely to chat. Bill, will you show me out, please."

At the doorstep I said under my breath, "Bill, how long has this been going on?"

"Oh, she's not been right for a long time," he replied. "But it's ramped up big time lately."

"What do you mean, ramped up?" I asked.

"Well, you know, all this carry on, with the voices, that's only just happened over the past week."

"What do you put it down to, Bill?" I enquired. "You know Joan better than anyone else."

"I don't know, Father. I've never known anything like this before. I don't know where to turn. When I saw you walk past it was like an answer to a prayer. I thought, I'll get some help now."

"Bill, you will get some help. But I'm not sure carrying on in your front room is the best way of getting it."

I reached out and put my hand on his shoulder to reassure him. "I will be back, I just need a rest and to talk to someone first."

Unlocking my door, I went straight to the kitchen, flipping on the coffee machine: I needed some fuel. I was spent. Joan's situation was beyond me and I needed to think the next move through. As I drank, I thought over the evening's events. I felt for Bill and Joan, their domestic life interrupted by a series of disturbing and increasingly violent episodes. I needed some outside perspective, but where could I turn?

There was Derek, an ex-journalist, now a vicar in Cheshire. He was somewhat of an authority on these matters, and had come across activity he couldn't explain or deal with in any other way during his ministry, but I was worried that the distance between us would preclude him from getting involved.

Then, out of left field, I remembered James, a particularly prayerful Christian. He wasn't ordained or even active in his local church, but he was one of the most prayerful people I'd met. He designed his garden specifically so he could sit and spend time in what he called "the presence of the Lord". He'd been involved in the early days of the deliverance ministry in our local area, and I thought it'd be worth talking to him.

"So, tell me Seth, was there any reaction to the name of Jesus?" James's voice was slow, measured and as warm as ever.

"There seemed to be, but not every time," I said, into the phone tethered to the kitchen wall in the days before cordless technology.

"There will always be a reaction to the name of Jesus if there are pigs in the parlour." This colloquialism was used by some of us after reading a book about the deliverance ministry with this title. "It doesn't have to be fire and brimstone. It could be anger, defiance, sadness even," James continued.

"James, I'm just not feeling it. I didn't get a consistent reaction to the name of Jesus. Plus, it felt almost staged."

"You mean it was set up?"

"No, not deliberately anyway. It felt like we were all playing the parts we were expected to play. You know, like when the mother-in-law comes round. You watch your p's and q's and steer the conversation round to safe topics."

"I get you now," James acknowledged. "So we're both agreed there isn't enough to say that genuine evil is present."

"Yes, I think so. I'm surer now I've spoken to you," I replied.

"Now listen, if we're right, you need to take care," James insisted. "No more mumbo jumbo. Revisit, but without any props or paraphernalia. You might make the situation far worse for them. It looks like it's a mental health issue. You must look for another cause." James didn't possess a formal qualification in theology, but his cool head, years of experience and Christian common sense were worth far more.

As I walked the short distance back to Bill and Joan's house, I felt far more confident than earlier. I was thinking about what James had said. What possible other cause could there be? Finding it might be easier said than done. Bill greeted my knock by opening the door and inviting me in. I steered us into the kitchen.

"How is she, Bill? "I asked.

"Mostly calm. There's been no more carry-on."

As we were speaking, I looked over Bill's shoulder and saw on the windowsill above the sink a wickerwork plant holder in the shape of a wheelbarrow, holding a spider plant. Either side of it were several brown plastic pill bottles.

"I hope you don't mind me asking Bill, but what are all those pills for?"

"Oh them?" He nodded in the direction of the sink. "They're Joan's."

"Joan's, what for?" I asked, "Do you mind me looking?" I motioned towards the pills and stepped forward before Bill could refuse.

"Them's for pain. In her back," he said, as I picked up a bottle and began to read. "She has arthritis in her bones." The label said codeine. "She might as well not bother with them," he continued bleakly.

"Why's that?" I asked.

"Well, they don't touch the pain when it's on her." He shook his head. "We've done everything the doctor said. Heat pads, ice pads, paracetamol, them things." He nodded at the bottle. "Nothing works."

"Bill, let me get this straight. Joan has arthritis in her back."

"The doctor said it's something else," he interrupted. "Beginning with O."

"Osteoporosis?" I suggested.

"Sounds right to me," he replied

"Then it will be painful, but these should make some difference." I shook the bottle.

"They don't even touch it. She might as well be chewing Smarties," he added.

This just didn't sit right with me. I had spent long enough in my father's pharmacy over the years listening to his sage advice to customers to know that this powerful opioid should at least take the edge off. Perhaps I was groping towards the "something else" James had advised me to find.

"Bill, I want you to promise to take Joan back to the doctor in the morning," I said. "Make a fuss, tell him what you've told me. She needs looking at. Ask for an appointment at the hospital. You need to get her to a specialist. Don't be put off, keep on at the doctor until he agrees. It's the squeaky hinge that gets the oil. She shouldn't be suffering like this."

"I… We don't like to make a fuss." I could see he was struggling to come to a decision. "But we can't carry on like this, can we?" His mind seemed to be made up and I left him to follow through on this resolve.

18 months later I was washing up; resting on the windowsill above my sink was a wickerwork plant holder in the shape of a wheelbarrow, holding a simple spider plant: my sole bequest from Joan. I always used to comment on it as we sat at her kitchen table drinking tea during my subsequent visits, until she finally passed away.

Osteoporosis is a terrible condition and leads to terrible pain, but Joan was suffering from something more sinister and malignant. An aggressive form of cancer was discovered during the hospital appointment that Bill had insisted the doctor refer Joan to.

It was a bitter discovery. There was to be no repeat of the strange episode of the stage-managed exorcism. With the right palliative care, Joan's pain was managed clinically and the psychological strain began to subside.

It has been documented that chronic pain can cause shifts in personality: when you stub your toe you might not be approachable for a moment or two. Imagine the impact of acute pain, day in and day out.

Joan's extreme behaviour was possibly a reaction to the extreme pain she was experiencing but does it fully explain the shift in her personality, the other entities seemingly taking control of her voice and actions? I don't know. I don't suppose I ever will, but I'm happy that the explanation rests within her brain, and not the spiritual realm.

What about her unnatural strength; surely that was an indication of something supernatural? Her ability to wrestle with two fit and strong grown men was indeed out of the ordinary, but was it supernatural? Well, the answer to that lies in something called disinhibition. Our minds and therefore our conscious actions are governed by social norms. What we consider to be right ensures that we very rarely lose control and use our strength to its fullest potential. Psychologists define it as a lack of restraint in complete disregard of social conventions, leading to impulsive behaviour and poor risk assessment.

If you've ever tried to pick up a toddler weighing just a few stone in the midst of a tantrum, you'll have some inkling of the strength of disinhibition. Now imagine an adult – even a five-foot-tall, seven-stone woman – and put them in the place of that toddler, then the display of strength we experienced that night might not be beyond the capabilities of the human body.

Despite the bizarre nature of this encounter, I look back on it with a measure of positivity. Out of what appeared to be a dark, even diabolic situation, some comfort was derived. Joan managed to see out the days remaining to her in control of herself, in her right mind, and with the love of her family around her.

Chapter 19

BOX GATE BLESSING

On a normal Thursday night, I closed my door, pulled up the drawbridge and was ready to relax. I put the kettle on, ready to reflect on the day and make a list of jobs for the next day. Once done, I could recover some peace of mind. I'd had enough for one day. Or so I thought. I didn't even get the chance to make that cup of tea, which I thought I thoroughly deserved after a day of parish ministry. While the kettle was still boiling, my phone rang. On the line was a man who sounded concerned.

"Hello, is that Father Seth," he enquired.

"Yes it is, how can I help?" I replied.

"It's hard to say," he hesitated, clearly unsure. "I didn't want to bother you, but it's our lass, she's more worried than I am."

"Worried, that doesn't sound good; what is it she's worried about?" I asked.

"Well, that's just it. I feel a fool talking about it like." He seemed reluctant to explain what was troubling him.

"Why not try me?" I tried to reassure him. "If it's led to you calling me, surely it can't be that foolish, can it?"

"Right oh, I'll come right out with it. We think there's something wrong with our house."

This piqued my curiosity; surely a plumber, electrician or builder should be their first port of call?

"Right. Okay." I was struggling to work out how to respond. "What do you think is wrong with the house?" I asked, reflecting the comment back to him.

"It's more our lass than me. I didn't want to bother you," he said apologetically. "But she won't let it go."

"Well, we have to do as we're told, don't we?" I answered, trying to get him on side. "What is it that's got your wife so worked up?"

"I'll come right out with it." *I wish you would*, I thought.

"My wife, my wife. Well, we think our house, well…" he stuttered, reluctant to say something which would probably make him sound ridiculous. "Well, it's haunted."

I'd half guessed it'd be something like this. His reluctance to speak clearly was an indicator that something out of the ordinary was behind it. But how does one reply to a statement like that?

The counselling module of my training for ministry came into its own and I reflected the statement back to him: "It's haunted, you say?"

This allowed me to place the onus on him to explain further without sounding judgmental.

"Aye, there's been some things happening that we can't work out like," he said.

"Like what? Can you give me an example or two of these things?" I asked evenly, trying hard not to convey any emotion. I didn't want to sound incredulous or even overly interested. It was important that I didn't contribute to the emotional momentum of the conversation and add any unwarranted credence to what was being said.

"Well, footsteps. We hear footsteps when there's no one else in the house". This sounded like it needed following up.

"Do you live in a detached house?" I asked.

"No, a semi, we're not posh, you know," he replied. "Why?"

"I'm just trying to build a picture," was my not entirely honest reply. The footsteps could quite easily be noise transmitted through the floors and walls from a neighbour in the adjoining property.

"We've also had drawers open like," he went on.

"What do you mean?" I pressed.

"Well, not me, but the wife has been in the spare room when a drawer in the dresser opened on its own."

"A new dressing table?" I asked, because floors are rarely flat in a property; carpets are raised by gripper strips on the edge of the floor. It's feasible that a modern dressing table with wheeled runners in the drawers might open if the rear legs are higher than the front. The vibrations of a footfall as someone walked past, or the action of someone sitting down on a nearby bed or chair might be enough to cause a drawer to open if it was on a slight downward angle.

"No, it's old. It were her mother's," was his reply. "But that's not all; our Sheba, that's my dog, won't go into that room. You can't even drag her in."

He was sounded increasingly agitated as he recounted what they believed they had been experiencing, but as there was no mention of threat or injury, I tried to put off a visit until the morning.

"Will someone be in around 10 in the morning?" I asked.

"Aye, my wife will. But can't you come tonight?" he pleaded.

"It's getting a bit late," I replied.

"I know, I wouldn't ask if we weren't getting a little bit desperate. It's more for my wife than for me; she's getting quite worked up about it."

I'm not sure I entirely bought the "It's my wife that's worried" spin; he sounded genuinely concerned and more than a little bit afraid.

It was clear their peace of mind was being affected. "Can you give me your address and I'll pop over in 10 minutes," I acquiesced.

The address was just outside our parish boundary. Now there's an etiquette to follow; I couldn't just enter a colleague's parish and minister to their flock; it wasn't on.

"But you're not in our parish, have you tried calling your vicar?" I asked, wanting to avoid stepping on anyone's toes.

"We've rung up three or four times this past week and left messages but no one's got back to us," he explained.

I remembered that my colleague in the next parish was on leave, but someone should've been checking his messages. I made a snap decision.

"I'll be over in 10 minutes."

Whatever was going on in that house was causing real stress and anxiety, and I wouldn't sleep if I didn't respond and try to help.

I wasn't sure what to think; on most occasions, supposed haunting activities have a rational explanation, whether accepted by those experiencing them or not. And just because a few anecdotal accounts couldn't be explained or dismissed, didn't mean the answer lay in the realm of the supernatural. Sometimes we just don't know what's taken place and we should leave it at that. The trouble is, people don't like the not knowing; we like certainty and aren't good at living with loose ends.

Do you have a friend or relative who likes to find the source of any illness? I have, and they're like a one-person environmental health department. If I have a stomach upset, they want to know what I've eaten and where I ate it. They normally proclaim take-away food to be the source of the infection and are happy to stop their inquisition. If I have a migraine, the questioning is around how many cups of coffee I've consumed, whether I ate cheese, am I stressed. I prefer to take my medication and retreat to my bed. No, some people are happy with any answer, even if they know it's wrong.

Anecdotal evidence is the hardest to explain away and I've given up even trying. When someone tells you they experienced a ghost flicking their hair whilst sat in a haunted pub, no rational explanation will be accepted. Some take it personally, as if by rejecting their explanation, you're rejecting or belittling them, so I try to affirm what they've experienced without accepting the explanation: it was real to them.

People have told me that a picture of a deceased loved one has fallen off the wall when they were talking about them: explain that! It's futile trying to logically work through any alternative explanation. In pointing out that they've probably talked about that loved one a thousand times and no picture has fallen off the wall before, you're bursting their bubble and denying them the little bit of excitement that adds colour to the mundane drudge of everyday life.

We are pattern-seeking creatures; we have an inbuilt need to make meaning, even when that meaning is not always the right one. How many times have you been thinking about someone and they've rung you or sent you a text? That is memorable. Less so are the 100s of times you you've been thinking about them and they *haven't* rung you or messaged you, and therefore you give it no significance.

BOX GATE BLESSING

I had no doubt I was going to a property where people had attributed the wrong meaning to these occurrences; they'd sought a pattern – and found it. By accepting those coincidences and happenings that supported the picture of the house being haunted and rejecting the explanations that showed it was not, they'd arrived at the wrong conclusion.

I worried that by turning up to bless the house, I was giving these foolish notions credence, but the die had been cast...

From the outside, it seemed to be an ordinary semi-detached house, identical to many on the Box Gate Estate, built as part of an government initiative between the world wars to cope with the burgeoning post-war baby-boom population. They'd been built to identical plans, and to a budget reflecting the austerity of that time.

The front door opened in response to my firm knock and I was greeted by the sight of a middle-aged, medium-built man, one hand on the door handle and the other the other holding the collar of a large German Shepherd dog. This, I presumed, was "our Sheba". I was invited inside and the dog was released; it sniffed me and seemed happy its owner was satisfied I was a friend, not a foe.

I declined the offer of a cup of tea, thinking that I'd be in and out of the place in 15 minutes at most. I was taken into the living room where the man's wife was seated on a sofa. She got up and shook my hand.

"Oh Father Seth, I'm so pleased that you could come," she gushed. "We came to a baptism at All Saints, and it was a lovely service."

"Thank you," I said as I sat down, my ego suitably polished. She knew how to work people.

"Would you mind telling me what it is you're worried about?" I asked.

"Well, first, I thought my mind was playing tricks on me. 'Don't be daft,' I said to myself when I started to hear the footsteps. But when he heard it, too, we knew that something was up. We've lived here for 25 years and we've never heard footsteps from next door before," she said, convinced.

I wondered whether their neighbours had perhaps taken up a carpet and laid a wooden floor in its place? But surely that's the sort of detail a long-term neighbour would have noticed. It doesn't take a curtain twitcher to spot a van from a carpet or flooring firm parked outside, or to hear construction work taking place.

"And then, when the drawer opened, that put the wind right up me." It was clear these experiences were real to her and had made her fearful. As she recounted them, she was wringing her hands, talking fast and had started to tremble.

"Take your time, it's alright," I tried to reassure her.

"I'm sorry, it's just such a relief to have someone to talk to about it who won't think I'm mad," she continued.

"When Sheba started growling, I thought there must've been a burglar in the house."

"Growling?" I asked.

"Yes, she started growling outside the spare room. She used to sleep in there in the daytime; it catches the sun late on and Sheba would lie where it was warm. But not anymore."

There is a common perception that animals are particularly sensitive to the presence of supernatural activity. Up to this point, I had no real experience of this.

"She won't go near that room anymore, sometimes she won't even go upstairs," she continued.

"Right." I'd heard enough and wanted to take the conversation in another direction. "I want to talk to you about the books we read and the films we watch and how they help to create an atmosphere in our home." I was convinced this was a case of people frightening themselves. "Do you like to watch horror films?"

"Oh no, nothing like that, it's not our cup of tea," she replied.

"I hope you don't mind me asking, it's just that in most cases like this people have read a book about a haunting, or watched a film with a similar theme," I explained. "It's not that they're making it up, but having read a book or watched a film containing supernatural happenings, it can lead to them thinking that the same thing is happening in their own house."

"Well that's not what's going on here," her husband interjected brusquely. "We're not like that."

Without meaning to, I had overstepped the mark and had some work to do to win him back on side. "I'm sorry, but it's my job to state the obvious sometimes. It clearly isn't the case here, but for other people it has been. Now, if it's okay with you, I will go into each room on my own and pray. When I've done that, I'd like to pray with you too, and that should settle things down."

I was still convinced that something had influenced their perception of what was happening in their house, but I was wary of pressing them any further.

I had brought my night prayers service booklet with me and I went from room to room reciting part of the liturgy and saying some of the prayers. There was nothing out of the ordinary; no noises, no sense of atmosphere, no foul odour, no unusual cold or heat: no indicators of supernatural activity.

I'd left the spare room until last.

It was here, at the doorway, that I started to feel different. It might have been better if I hadn't been told that the problems were focused on this room. As a skeptic, I know that having that knowledge could have allowed a sense of anticipation to build. I wasn't able to approach that room in an objective manner; I'd been cued to expect the supernatural, and that sense of anticipation brought with it a sense of fear.

BOX GATE BLESSING

I entered, turned the light on and was greeted with the sight of a room that didn't fit in with the style of the rest of the property. The decor and furniture all seemed 30 years older, as if it had been kept back a generation. It was a small room with just enough space for a double bed, a wardrobe, a chest of drawers and a dressing table opposite the bottom of the bed. I positioned myself in the gap between the bed and dressing table and began to recite this prayer: "Visit, we implore thee, O Lord, this dwelling, and thrust from it all the traps of our foes."

As I got to this line, I was doubled up by a spasm of pain which contracted my chest and drove the breath from my lungs. I fell to my knees as my vision started to blur and I felt the room growing dark. It passed as quickly as it had come; I stood up, shook my head, regained my composure and continued.

"Let thy sacred cherubs reside here to keep us in peace; and may thy eternal blessing remain here amongst us, through Jesus Christ our Lord. Amen."

With the "Amen", the door, which was partly closed, flew open as Sheba bounded into the room. Her tail wagged vigorously as she jumped up at me. She was quickly followed by the man and his wife. Both had looks of concern which turned to smiles when they saw that Sheba had lost her fear of the room and had made a new friend in me.

Over a cup of tea after I'd prayed with the couple in the living room, I asked a question which I knew I had to ask. I couldn't go home until I had satisfied my curiosity: "Why is the spare room set out so differently from the rest of the house?"

"Well, it was for your mother, wasn't it love?" The man motioned to his wife.

"Yes, she wasn't right well and she came to stay with us. She couldn't manage in her own place and we wanted to make her feel at home, so she brought some of her things with her."

"Right, so why isn't she with you now?" I asked.

"Well, she died about 18 months ago," the woman said, looking down at the floor.

"I'm sorry to hear that," I said.

"Yes, she had heart disease for a few years. It started with angina and just got worse. Then one day I were down here making a cup of tea and I heard a bang from upstairs and thought that she'd dropped something heavy. I called up the stairs to her but didn't get a reply. So I went up. And that's when I found her. She'd had a heart attack and died on the spot. I'll never forget finding her laid out there between the bed and the dresser."

I finished my tea and left soon after with much food for thought. I was never called out to that house again. I can only surmise that the disturbances, whatever they had been, had ceased.

This remains for me the one incident I have difficulty rationalising. As I review it, I have to question the chest pain I'd felt. Was it real? Was it just a passing spasm that occurred at the right time for me to attach some meaning to it? Had I been told about the death in the room before I came upstairs and not after, as I remember it? What about the dog? Why had Sheba been reluctant to enter that room for so long, then suddenly, after that bizarre incident during the prayer, why had she bounded into the room and seemed so happy to be there?

I don't suppose I'll ever have answers; I still puzzle over what took place and sometimes wonder whether there's some evidence somewhere in the details of this incident that should make me more cautious and think again about my atheism.

Was this a drama where all the players knew their part and acted accordingly, or were there other forces at work? Saint Paul wrote that our struggle isn't against flesh and blood, but principalities and powers, the rulers of the dark forces of our world. I wasn't convinced of this, but Sheba sensed a change in that house and every afternoon, when the sun's shining, she finds her way back to the little room and falls asleep in the warmth of the afternoon sunlight.

Chapter 20

ICE LOLLY SUICIDE

On a sunny spring morning, I was taking advantage of my flexible working schedule to do the weekly grocery shop. I lived mainly alone, so was able to please myself, not having to fit my schedule around that of a significant other.

Part of my role was to be available around the clock for my flock. As a consequence, I didn't have a set working schedule. Yes, there were regular weekly services to attend, routine clergy meetings, home Communions and the ad hoc addition to my schedule of funerals and hospital visits. But it meant I could pick the time when I shopped. Not for me the tussle of a packed shop on a Saturday morning; midweek and part-way through the working day, the supermarket was relatively customer free.

Due to the unseasonably warm weather, the ice cream aisle seemed more than usually attractive. I selected a box of ice lollies, rationalising that I'd be home in 10 minutes and able to get them into the freezer. With my shop completed, I began the journey home.

As I drove, I don't know why, but my thoughts turned to Cecil. He was in his early 30s, recently separated from his wife and extremely active in the life of the church. He was also clearly troubled.

At times he dressed in strange, loose-fitting garments. The skin on his hands and lower arms was often sore and cracked. At first, I believed he suffered from eczema, or some similar skin complaint, but I'd begun to doubt this. I hadn't joined the dots yet, but a picture of a disturbed young man was emerging. Something was making Cecil deeply unhappy. When you're in reasonably close proximity to someone, you often catch their individual scent. With Cecil, all I could detect was the taint of chlorine. I'd wondered whether he was a keen swimmer.

As I drove past the church on the way home, I spotted Cecil's house on a narrow lane running parallel to the churchyard. I had a growing conviction I should call on him. I thought that as soon as I'd unpacked my shopping I'd turn round, come back up to the church, park my car and walk the short distance to see him.

But as I drove further away from his house, I began to feel agitated and uncomfortable. A conviction was growing inside me that I had to turn round and see him immediately. I dismissed it as plain fancy; my boot was full of groceries and, with the whole afternoon free, I could go and see him once I'd put them away. In the end, I gave in, turned into a side road and headed back up towards the church.

I parked in the churchyard and knocked on Cecil's door. There was no response. I knocked again. No response. This was just stupid. I felt foolish I'd given in to this urge. Why had I turned round and wasted precious free time coming here?

I was about to leave when, through the obscured glass of the front door, I noticed movement inside the house.

I knocked for a third time and waited. The movement was coming closer to the front door. It opened a crack, just wide enough for Cecil to peer out at me.

"Hello Cecil, I just called round to say hello and see if your kettle is working," I said cheekily.

The door opened wider and I entered the house. It was immaculate, sparsely decorated with just a few belongings. I then realised that the smell of chlorine wasn't due to Cecil swimming, it was the pervasive aroma of bleach: the house reeked of it. With a blinding flash of realisation it came to me: Cecil was in the vice-like grip of obsessive-compulsive disorder. Unlike the type I suffered from as a child, his was based on contamination and cleanliness. It would have entailed repeated personal washing, explaining the cracked, sore skin and loose-fitting clothes. It would also account for his immaculate house.

I followed him through to the kitchen. He hadn't said a word to me so far. He bent down to the floor, picked up several cooking utensils and a large bread knife and dropped them into the sink, which was filled with water mixed with bleach.

He filled the kettle, switched it on and turned to face me for the first time since I'd arrived. His eyes were red-rimmed and his cheeks were moist with tears.

"You must think I'm stupid," he said, full of self-loathing. "I don't like anyone seeing me cry."

"Of course I don't," I replied as I took a step towards him, then checked my progress. My first thought was to physically comfort him, but if his OCD was associated with contamination and cleanliness, then I might trigger cleaning rituals that would cause him a lot of distress.

"Cecil, you're far from happy. Do you want to talk about it?" I asked.

"No, I do not. It's none of your business anyway." He seemed angry towards me.

I felt embarrassed. I had pushed too hard too soon and had done more harm than good. Perhaps a dignified retreat was in order?

"I can see you're upset and don't want to talk about it. Is it okay if we pray?" I suggested.

He broke down at this, his shoulders rising and falling as he was consumed with grief. I waited. The sobbing began to subside.

"I'm sick of it. I'm sick of it all."

Only those who have been locked in the prison of obsessive-compulsive disorder can truly understand the loathing you feel towards your rituals. I understood, because I had shared the despair he was experiencing.

"I know," was all I could say.

"You know nothing about me. You know nothing about it," was his bitter reply.

"I do," I replied evenly. "I had number rituals which I had to carry out in a certain way. If not, I had to carry them out squared."

"Squared?" he asked, his curiosity piqued.

"Yes. Squared. Mine were based on sets of five. I had to count one, two, three, four and then finish with one again. I might be leaving the house, but it had to be done five times. If I didn't do it right, it would be 25 times or even 125 times. It was a lot for a little boy to carry," I explained. "So, you see, I know. I might not know all you're having to do, but I know enough to see that it's awful for you."

A silence hung in the air. I could see that Cecil was thinking about what I'd said.

"I think you do know, don't you?" he asked, almost looking for some hope. "And you stopped?"

"Yes I did," I replied.

"How did you stop?" His question seemed genuine.

"I just felt like I'd had enough. I couldn't go on anymore," I continued. "I was nine and I was in the middle of walking through my school door for the 125th time and I got angry. Angry for being held a prisoner to the rituals, angry for all those bad thoughts, isolation and wasted childhood. It welled up from deep inside me and I shouted "stop!" at the top of my voice. If anyone had been bothered to notice me, they'd have thought I'd gone mad. That was the beginning of the end. It took months of effort, but it eventually stopped."

A few years before this incident, I had a moment of epiphany about my childhood OCD. I hadn't known what it was, or what it was called. I'd studied a mental health medical text book to help me understand some of the situations I was in, and why some of the people I was now dealing with sometimes exhibited such extreme behaviour.

The chapter on OCD shed considerable light on my issues as a young boy and would help in this situation with Cecil. I was becoming increasingly convinced that most of the issues I was confronted with were rooted in the mind and not the soul. Medical theory was becoming more relevant to my ministry than the Bible. I'm saddened no adult noticed me or offered some help when I was suffering from OCD. I think that's why I notice the signs in others. OCD is insidious; its roots find their way into every hidden nook and cranny of your life, leaving you with nothing. When it has possession of you, it starts to drive a wedge between you and the outside world. Your behaviours become such a source of shame and self-loathing that eventually you begin to withdraw into youself to hide them from others. The lucky ones are those who reach rock bottom and haven't got the strength to carry on. They come to realise they should loathe their obsession rather than themselves, and that's the beginning of the path to release. Someone once said that a man without hope is a man without fear, and this is the point that Cecil had arrived at.

"I want it to stop," he said. "But I can't make it stop." His head sagged. "Do you know what I was doing when you knocked on the door?"

"No, tell me."

"I was in the kitchen, in my knife drawer; I was choosing which one would be the best for cutting my throat. You knocked. I thought if I ignored it, you might go away and I could end it. But you didn't, you kept knocking."

I spent a long time with Cecil that day. I heard about his journey into oppression and how rejection had led him down this path. He spoke of desperate attempts to seek help, but to no avail. He had been exploited by a cult in a nearby city, which, like most predators, had sniffed his vulnerability out and drawn him in with fake friendship, lies and financial demands. He had reached rock bottom and was at his wit's end when I called round.

When I finally returned to the vicarage to pack away my groceries, I was spent, and my ice lollies were ruined.

A chance encounter with Cecil a year after my release from faith made me smile then, and it still makes me smile today. I was shopping in the town centre and Cecil appeared at my elbow. He was beaming and clearly happy. He had been clothes shopping for an outfit to wear to a friend's wedding. There was no sign of obsession or compulsion, depression or self-loathing; only warmth and a smile that couldn't be faked.

Sometimes in life we all act on a whim, or an inner conviction. We might not know where it comes from, but its insistent nagging forces us to act. In this case and at this time I was able to help someone living an oppressed life. I'll never forget what happened that day, and I hope that Cecil has indeed left his rituals behind and has the freedom to live his life in the peace that he deserves.

Chapter 21

RUNNING ON EMPTY

My new parish was near the local hospital, a great advantage as it meant only a short journey to visit any sick parishioners.

It also had its drawbacks: when members of the chaplaincy team were unavailable, the staff would ring round the nearest parishes, putting me in the frame for sure.

In the early hours of the morning, I was roused from sleep by the insistent ringing of my telephone. I wandered downstairs in the dark, my feet chilled by the cold kitchen floor, and picked up the receiver.

"Hello, Saint Joseph's vicarage, Father Seth speaking," I mumbled, as brightly as I could manage.

"Hello Father." Whoever was speaking was more awake than me. "I got your number from one of our staff members who came to your church to have their daughter baptised." This was beginning to sound interesting.

"They said that you might be able to help us with the family who are here with us." And here she paused, prompting me to respond, "Well, I'll do my best."

"I'm sure you will," she said. "They have a daughter who's a few days old. She is very poorly and we have made the decision to switch her life support off," she explained carefully. It was clear that members of the family were within earshot. I was now fully awake, my nerves jangling. "They'd like their daughter to be christened before the end," she explained.

"Of course I will come and help. But what about the chaplaincy team? I don't want to tread on anyone's toes," I explained.

"We rang and left messages on answer machines, but no one got back to us." She sounded harassed. "We need to do this sooner rather than later."

"I'll be there in 15 minutes," I pledged, and returned the receiver to its cradle.

I've previously spoken about the added weight that ministry can place on your shoulders, about the emotional drag, which means that each day can bring a sense of mental and emotional drain.

I was in the grip of a downward spiral at this point. I'd underestimated the damage to my faith that in-depth Bible study had caused. I remember asking the chaplain at theological college about a difficult passage in the Bible. I was having problems reconciling what was written with my concept of God as a loving, merciful and just being.

It is a ridiculous incident, recorded in two verses of the Old Testament, but it was the beginning of the crumbling of the dam of my faith. A great prophet is walking to the town of Bethel, when some boys came out of the town and jeer at him. He curses them in the name of the Lord, and two bears come out of the woods and maul 42 of the boys. As stupid as it sounds, these verses may have been the beginning of my journey into atheism.

The chaplain's response to my doubts failed to shore up my faith: "Well you see, Walker, times were hard in those days", hardly seemed adequate.

As the years progressed, and my faith became tested first at Bluebell Common, Brinsley, and then my third parish, I wasn't 100 per cent sure I believed any more.

I took my time to get dressed and gather some orders of service and christening cards before driving towards the hospital.

The special-care baby unit, was, like most children's wards, brightly decorated and kitted out with all kinds of toys, books and pictures.

However, there was to be no playing on this occasion. An ashen-faced father and a sob-wracked mother supported by a senior nurse made up the congregation. The baby, scarcely bigger than a doll, had been disconnected from various machines, wires and tubes. The nurse had dressed her in what was probably the outfit she would've worn to come home from hospital.

I asked for a bowl of water, handed out orders of service, took the baby in my arms and, as the physical signs of life faded, carried out one of the most difficult, poignant and excruciating services I'd ever conducted.

A christening is usually an exuberant, joyful occasion, a celebration of new life and a welcoming into the family of the church. Not on this occasion. The only sounds were my voice, the sobbing of the parents and the bleeping of medical apparatus. My heart was wrenched for the family and I felt bitter regret for the wasted potential I held in my hands.

Where was God in all this?

Within an hour I was back at the vicarage, brewing a pot of strong coffee. Shellshocked would be a good description.

I was too numb to try to make sense of what I'd just been a part of. I had proclaimed God's love to a father and mother from whom he had taken the most treasured and anticipated gift.

The dam was breached and I wept. Like a tree in autumn, the leaves of my faith that had made up my personal identity and were the foundation of my being were slowly shrivelling up and falling away.

I was to get an inkling of what this couple faced some 20 years later, when my wife and I attended the same hospital for a pre-natal scan. This was our second child, an addition we hoped would complete our family.

The operator of the ultrasound scanner was bright and upbeat. My wife lay on the couch with her abdomen exposed. The lighthearted comment about the gel applied to the scanner head being cold drew polite smiles. I'd paid £5 for a scan image printout, for the obligatory social media post and announcement. As the scanner head met my wife's tummy, an image of the small jellybean-shaped fetus appeared. I smiled as I strained to make out the potential life which would become intimately meshed into our existing family.

"Hmmph…"

The sonographer exhaled through her nose. I turned my attention from screen to operator. The smile was gone; her thin lips were pressed together and she was frowning. She seemed to be struggling to come to a decision. She reached up and switched the monitor off. My wife and I looked at each other, not knowing what was going on.

"Will you excuse me a minute," she asked. "I'm just going to speak with my colleague."

I reached for my wife's hand and gave it a squeeze.

We didn't really know what to say to each other. It was clear that something wasn't right. My wife cleaned the gel from her stomach with a paper towel from a roll fixed to the wall. She rearranged her clothes and sat upright on the gurney while we waited in silence.

Our heads swivelled towards the door in unison when it opened to reveal a middle-aged woman in a floral print dress. No uniform, just a badge.

"Mr and Mrs Walker, I'm Jane Simpson, the lead consultant for the unit. I need to talk to you about the scan. Please," she beckoned. "Would you follow me?"

I didn't want to follow her. I didn't want to hear what she had to say. It wasn't going to be good, that was for sure.

We entered a sparsely appointed, but neat room. It was clearly set out for such conversations. There was no office clutter, no posters featuring families, children, or mothers holding babies.

"As you may be aware, we scan at this stage in the pregnancy for various conditions. One of the tests we do is to measure something called nuchal thickness, that is the width of a fluid-filled sac on the back of the fetus's neck. Anything up to three millimetres shouldn't cause us any concern. As we get closer to six there is an increasing indication of a problem."

We were both nodding, as we were well aware of the significance of her words. As older parents – my wife was approaching 40 and I was 50 – you tend to read up to prepare yourselves for what might happen.

"The thickness we detected on this fetus is 13 millimetres. A thickness over 6.5 is usually an indication of a chromosomal abnormality such as Down's Syndrome. We would like to transfer you to the City Children's Hospital, as they have a specialist provision and could better meet your needs. They'll be able to provide you with more information after a different type of scan.

They might also remove part of the placenta to carry out some tests to rule out chromosomal abnormalities. However, the indications are that the fetus won't reach full term."

I don't remember leaving the hospital or the journey home. I was numb. Was I tempted to revive my faith and beg God for help? No, I wasn't. This was, for me, further confirmation of his lack of existence. A loving God wouldn't afflict a fetus in the womb, would he?

Within 24 hours we found ourselves sitting in the waiting room in the City Children's Hospital 20 miles away. I'm not sure either of us had got much sleep, but we were determined to get some more information.

A further scan revealed that the fluid-filled sac was likely to be a cystic hygroma – a cyst – which extended from the top of the back of the head all the way down the back and the left arm. Part of the placenta was taken away for testing, a painful procedure for my wife which came with a risk of miscarriage.

We were told that from the thickness alone, there was a high chance the fetus had Down's Syndrome or Edwards Syndrome. The scan had detected that blood was flowing round the heart the wrong way: 'Reverse Flow in Ductus Venosus' was the term used. 80 per cent of Downs fetuses have this, we were informed, but 3 per cent of 'chromosomally usual' babies also have reverse flow.

This was not looking good.

There was also a high probability of a serious heart defect so a Doppler scan was booked in. We were counselled about the possibility of a termination.

Reflecting on this time is difficult for me. I don't mean because of the raw emotions; I mean because I have no emotional connection to it. I don't remember it with sadness, fear or any sense of anxiety. Although these were absolutely all present at the time, I can't access how I felt then, from my perspective today. The reason may become apparent as I continue the story.

My wife and I spoke at length about what we'd do. When we'd finished crying, we pulled ourselves together for the sake of each other and our five-year-old son.

Although we had no well of faith to draw on, we were convinced that we should give whatever was inside my wife's womb every chance of making it. We both agreed that if there was an 88 per cent chance that the fetus that would become our child would have a chromosomal abnormality, there was also a 12 per cent chance it would not. And what would we do if we knew the child did have some sort of issue? Well, I suppose we'd do what we'd always done in the 17 years we'd been together. We'd assess the situation, look at our available resources, have a hug, roll up our sleeves and get on with it.

We returned a few days later for the result of the placenta sampling. There was some good news. They had ruled out Down's Syndrome, Edwards Syndrome, Turner

Syndrome, Patau Syndrome and Noonan Syndrome. We were ecstatic, and it showed. However, the consultant wasn't as jubilant; the presence of the fluid was likely to be a sign that there was still some serious problem, like a heart defect.

We were advised cystic hygroma babies didn't always make it to full term if the fluid hadn't resolved by week 20, when the chance of a healthy outcome decreases to 2–9 per cent.

Even though a bleak picture had been painted, we decided that we could take that and be happy for now. We'd ruled out the most serious problems and were ready for the next challenge.

Two weeks later, we returned for the Doppler scan, which would indicate if there was a problem with our child's heart. There, you see? A change had happened; we no longer thought of it as a fetus, it was now a child, our child and we would do all we could to make sure they became part of our family.

The return visit to hospital was successful. No heart defect was detected and the reverse flow of blood had corrected itself.

We felt justified in taking the action we had. By waiting, we had given our child the chance it needed. If nature had taken its course and we'd lost him or her, it would have been easier to cope than if we'd decided to terminate and were worrying whether we'd made the right decision. These choices are individual and personal, and no blame, shame or pain is attached to any difficult decision anyone else has been forced to make.

Uncharacteristically, I had started to wonder, why us? I'm not one for regrets, for mulling over bad decisions I've made and wishing for better outcomes. However, I needed to understand why we had all these markers for a chromosomal abnormality, and yet test after test was telling us there wasn't one. And then it hit me like a bolt out of the blue. Darier disease.

I'd been diagnosed with this condition some 10 years previously. After a series of misdiagnoses stretching over a decade, I'd insisted my GP refer me to a dermatologist. A biopsy was taken from the affected area, tests were carried out and a diagnosis was made. It's a sufficiently rare genetic condition for mine to be the only case my doctor would see in his career. Around one in 70,000 people have it, but mine's an even rarer form. It's an inherited skin condition in which the cells in the outer layer of the skin lose the sticky junctions that hold them together. The result can be dramatic in appearance, foul in smell and debilitating due to the appearance of the rash.

Through the power of the web, I am part of a small community of people diagnosed with Darier; we tend to know more than our doctors, and sometimes more than the dermatologists who treat us. Some of what we believe is backed by research, some by our common experience.

We're aware of other impacts on us beyond the condition of our skin, the most significant being that nearly two thirds of us suffer from depression.

The Journal of the American Academy of Dermatology published a study which discovered that 7 out of 11 people with Darier had planned or attempted suicide, compared to 3 out of 11 in a control group. Some people argue that the depression is a result of our skin condition and the effects of an outbreak. I've seen some research which shows that the gene site affected also has some influence on our moods.

My wife can predict my outbreaks by my grumpiness. I'm not aware that I'm experiencing a mood change, but those around me are, and within a few days the tell-tale rash will begin to appear.

At our next pre-natal appointment, I spoke to the consultant about my genetic abnormality, and asked whether that could be a trigger for the supposed signs of a chromosomal abnormality. They weren't sure; the condition was so rare they had no way of linking it. However, our details were taken, and we were entered into a research study that may help others in the future to make a more informed choice.

Before we knew it, we were at our week 20 scan. Unfortunately for us, the nuchal thickness was still over 10 millimetres, indicating there was very little chance of a 'completely normal' child, whatever that meant.

If by week 24 the final scan showed t the thickness had reduced, then the odds would have moved in our favour.

However, at week 24, due to the position of the fetus and the lack of space due to its size, no measurement could be taken,

so a shadow was cast over the last few months of the pregnancy.

As time progressed, we prepared for the birth, but always worried it wouldn't happen, or that some problem would accompany it.

My wife was refused a natural birth, as a medicalised birth required attendance at the maternity unit

My wife felt the first contraction on the eve of the date she'd calculated for the birth, several days away from that given by the hospital. We knew from our first child that it'd be a quick process; he was born just four hours after the first contraction.

I dropped our son off with friends and returned to pick up my wife. As we drove out of our valley towards the hospital in a neighbouring town, my wife told me the contractions were now happening every 29 seconds. We live in the foothills of the Pennines and were driving through desolate moorland. I dialled for an ambulance and after going through the time-consuming questionnaire of symptoms, was told they couldn't dispatch an ambulance to us until we could provide a street name and number. My wife clamped down and I sped to the nearest village.

It was 1:30 in the morning and the streets were deserted. When I gave them a house number and street name, the dispatcher informed me no ambulances were available in our area but one was being dispatched from a city 15 miles away.

My wife said the baby was ready: our child was going to be born in the next few seconds. I hung up, opened the passenger door and removed my wife's pants just in time to clamp my hands around my new son's ankles as he came shooting out. It was like trying to grasp a flapping trout, and I just managed to stop him hitting the footwell. Turning him around in my arms I looked for any defects, for this fluid-filled sac. There were none: he was perfect. I placed him in my wife's arms and piled coats on top of them as we waited for the ambulance to arrive.

Six years on, we have a beautiful, intelligent and gregarious child. All he has to show for those months of worry is a slightly wider than normal neck. Will he inherit my Darier disease? Perhaps, yes. The chances are 50-50 and as we have one child who's disease free, the odds are against him. But we've heard that said before…

I sometimes wonder if I would've been a better pastor if I'd come to the ministry in later life. Would my experiences have changed the way I approached people? Undoubtedly, but would my faith have remained intact and fit enough for sharing? Probably not.

Twenty-five years ago I was serving in my third parish and beginning to run on empty. A few short weeks after the baptism in the special-care baby unit, I found myself officiating at a child's funeral. She was only four years old and had been taken by an aggressive form of cancer. It was devastating for the parents, and the wider family, too.

What could I say in the face of such suffering and grief? Could I suggest that their child had been spared far worse suffering in the future? Perhaps. Was it true? I doubt it, given the months of pain and suffering the child had endured. I decided to say as little as possible about why it had happened, and just focus on the little life she'd enjoyed and the love she'd brought to her family. As I prayed, I felt little certainty.

A few days later, we gathered at the graveside and released helium balloons as we prayed. Her siblings were told that the balloons would rise up to her and she could play with them. I went home, took off my dog collar and cried. This once sought-after symbol of ministry which I thought would open so many doors for me was instead closing in on me, constricting me. It was a visible reminder of my hypocrisy, as day by day my faith dwindled.

Chapter 22

THE FALL

I had reached a point where living a lie had started to undermine my personality. Earlier on I discussed the concept of personas, that we all have different ways of presenting ourselves to different people, or in different situations. For me, this had become something more concrete. It was no longer a way of behaving appropriately in certain circumstances; instead, I felt that I was fracturing into distinct personalities which were starting to conflict with each other. My faith had gone, but I still conducted worship, praying to a God I no longer believed in, whilst my skepticism sneered at the hypocrite I'd become.

I was increasingly sad, but became expert at hiding it from those around me. I needed a way out, but I couldn't find one. I had known no other world other than the family of the church and felt that I had nothing else to offer. I applied for a distance-learning course to gain a degree in a different discipline, in the hope that I could retrain as a teacher. I knew I could apply to train as a religious studies teacher, but I needed to walk away totally, to leave faith and all its trappings behind, but this course would see my crisis being waved in front of my face every working day.

I was also driven by the shame of what people would think about me. I was the one sibling who had embraced Christianity. More than that, I had entered the ministry. How could I face my parents again if I walked away from it all?

As my licensed tenure came to an end, I actively sought out a role that had little, if no, pastoral responsibilities.

I was appointed to an advisory role and relieved of all pastoral duties. I didn't share my reasons but explained that I felt I couldn't serve a parish effectively whilst conducting my other role, the regional oversight of colleagues from several dioceses. This was accepted and I was given an extended period of rest between appointments, but I didn't manage a single day in my new post.

I had hoped to feel some sense of relief, knowing that I would not have to minister to people's needs from a position of spiritual desolation. I'd bsupposedly been standing in place of God for the congregation and I didn't even believe in him. The term vicar comes from the Latin *vicarius*; it means a substitute, to quite literally stand in the place of God. Surely now, a chance to breathe, to recover, would help me shake the dust from my shoulders and move forward positively?

But it didn't. My hypocrisy clung to me like Marley's chains, and my regrets over my rotten choices became constant companions and sang songs of despair to me.

As the weeks went by, I sank further into a pit of depression. It would take four more years to gain another degree, studying part time. I needed an exit now and couldn't seem to see a way out.

As each night stretched into an infinity of wakefulness, tears and panic attacks, I sought control, some way of making it all stop.

I remember reaching into a kitchen drawer and taking a paring knife. There, in the darkness of the early hours, I cut at my chest. A mere graze. A sharp intake of breath as the red stripe appeared; the flash of pain brought momentary relief. By the time I'd finished painting, I'd carved a crimson lattice on the canvas of my torso.

The relief was intense but fleeting, and when my regrets returned, they brought their favourite companion with them: guilt. I was no stranger to guilt, but this time it was different, deeper, darker and it felt heavy as it wrapped its dread tentacles around me and pulled me further down into the shadows.

What had I done? What had I become? What was I becoming?

Years of work on myself has helped me to understand how every step of my life had led up to this point. I now know what to look out for, how to check my drift and to take charge of my own destiny, but back then I was rudderless and floundering. This was a journey which had offered a myriad of possible outcomes, so how did I end up there? Many factors brought me to that point, but the most important were of my own making: my choices, or rather my recurring inability or unwillingness to make good choices.

I'd failed to take charge of my life, I'd drifted, I'd lived the life I thought I was meant to, and most importantly I'd given far too much weight to what other people thought about me. The irony was that other people were probably not that bothered about my choices, and if they were, they'd have wanted me to be happy, wouldn't they?

Day after day I carried on, but inside it felt like I was walking through treacle. Every step was an effort; my painted smile was forced with an exertion that exhausted me. It's hard to describe how isolated I felt; it was as if I was a prisoner within my own body. As I talked with friends, the real me, imprisoned inside my shell, looked out and wept. It felt as though I was trapped behind a thick, opaque glass wall and could see a sunlit world of people through the mist, getting on with their lives. I could scream and bang on the walls, but no one could see or hear the wretch I'd become.

Looking back now, from a place of balanced mental health, surrounded by love, it's hard to remember how far I had journeyed into selfish loneliness.

FAITHLESS

I like to run over the moors: it's part of who I am now. Two or three times a week I set out, often from my own back door, and lose myself in nature. Sometimes I have a map, but 22 years in my valley means that the map has moved from backpack to memory.

Sometimes I run far. I mean far. On my 50th year I set out run between the highest points of six counties. While reconnoitering the route over several months, I was out of my comfort zone, in unfamiliar territory. The gap between the second and third county peak was 18 miles, much of it open moorland. I relied on map and compass, but on one barren stretch of peat moor, my navigation failed. I was just a few degrees off, but after a mile, those few degrees saw me entering the wrong clough, a small valley which led me in the wrong direction. It looked like the clough on the map, and there was a trod, a small path. I followed it. Anything was better than the endless heather bashing and bog hopping. Within 20 minutes I was nearly two miles from where I should have been. When I realised my mistake, I had to choose whether to descend a steep-sided valley and climb another hill – a climb my legs didn't have in them – or backtrack and carry on. That day's learning changed how I run; now, when I'm in unfamiliar territory, I always take the time to check whether I'm making a good navigation choice. A few degrees off over a distance has consequences, sometimes serious.

Looking back, I can see how, throughout my life, a failure to check my progress often nudged me in the wrong direction.

Bad choices made while navigating through life's twists and turns had sent me down a path which, ultimately, saw me lost, alone and a long way from where I should have been.

Each night was an eternity of self-loathing. I was experiencing a recurring dark night of the soul and I could see no way out, until, that is, the night that changed everything. I wrote the opening chapter describing the events of my rebirth fresh from coming to terms with who I'd become and what I'd done to myself and those closest to me. It was an important part of my journey to recovery, although sharing it comes with an emotional cost. I have taken my licks, healed my wounds and learned my lessons.

Like my father before me, I've had to start afresh, rebuilding my career and life in a new location. There've been dark times, but I've never returned even to the outer fringes of the desolation I once experienced. What's different? How have I managed to arrest this slide into oblivion? Well, through an honest look at where I was, why I was there and what I needed to do to move forward.

Sometimes it hasn't been easy to realise that I've started to drift off course; I've begun to slip – but I haven't fallen over again.

Hanging on my garage wall is my father's old ice axe. It isn't his oldest one, the one he used when climbing in the Dolomites in the 1950s, but it's last one he owned. I remember climbing with him in the Alps when I was 16. We were going to attempt Mount Blanc, but a week earlier I'd fallen 10 feet down a steep bank, jarring my spine. I couldn't risk pushing myself so soon after an injury, so we were limited to smaller challenges. We cut steps in the icy flank of a less formidable peak and practised glissading down the steep slopes. I started to lose control on one slide; I was using my ice axe as a friction brake to slow my slide, but it became ineffective as my momentum increased. "Arrest! Arrest!" my father shouted.

I instantly flipped over onto my front; grasping the head of the axe, I pushed the wide, blunt blade down with increasing force. As it bit into the ice, I pushed harder and eventually came to a safe halt.

I'm normally aware when I'm starting to slip in life, and I put the brakes on. When there is potential for me to make a wrong choice, when I don't realise I've started to slide, I have someone who loves me on hand to shout "Arrest! Arrest!" and help me back onto my feet.

Chapter 23

THE RISING

It's hard to understand the part I played in my own recovery compared to the contribution of those around me. I drifted for two months, running the risk of falling back down the slope to the old familiar pit of despair. Good counsel and firm guidance saw me applying for a post-graduate qualification, and, my lesson well and truly learnt, I set a direction for my life and followed it with determination and commitment.

In just over a year I'd gained my first more advanced qualification and within another year I was lecturing at university in what was a new discipline for me, helping to shape future educators. It was as if the wind had filled my sails and my hand was firmly on the rudder of my life. My motivation had moved away from erroneously trying to please those around me, including a disapproving God, and I was free to explore the endless possibilities that life has to offer. I took every opportunity that came my way; my mantra was push the door; if it opens, step inside and smile. This ethos has seen me travel to the far side of the world, talking with government officials about the future of education, visiting schools, universities and special-needs provisions to see the great work taking place in order to enrich our own learning.

As the years progressed, I found myself increasingly involved in consultancy work, helping to develop new qualifications to better prepare young people for the workplace of tomorrow. This wasn't easy, involving visits to London, long days pouring over specifications and sample examination papers, but it was rewarding, helping me to keep fresh and avoid the temptation to stagnate. I enjoyed the cut and thrust of life within this sector, but something was missing. I gained further post-graduate qualifications and became a verifier for action research papers within the education sector. It was stimulating to review the new ways of learning that educators were developing and trialling and I gained much from it. However, I was beginning to miss the personal touch. A travelling preacher who prayed over me when I was 15 said that the Lord had given me a pastor's heart, that I'd be a shepherd looking after God's flock. I don't believe for one minute this was a message from God, but he'd weighed my character up well. It was this pastoral element that was missing from my life and I felt it keenly.

As I hit my 50s, I took the opportunity like many of my colleagues to change direction again and move to a way of working that enabled me to control my diary better, to retain an overview of provision for some of the most vulnerable in society, but also to maintain and in some ways develop the pastoral aspects I'd missed so much. I developed an audit tool that enables an educational setting to identify their pupils' exact areas of vulnerability, helping them towards better provision, but I really wanted to be the one actually helping those with vulnerabilities.

As the years progressed, I steered my working life towards dealing with people again rather than papers. I frequently work to help repair dysfunctional teams and broken individuals; that's largely what I do today. I work with vulnerable people, and I also work with those who help vulnerable people.

My life has been far from smooth; there've been plenty of bumps to negotiate over the past two and a half decades, but it has been good. By taking responsibility for my direction and by not drifting, by taking the opportunities and pushing at the doors of opportunity, I have risen.

EPILOGUE

On a grey wet January morning, 30 years after leaving Bluebell Common, I was heading back to say my goodbyes to Gloria. The matriarch of the village had died in her 10th decade, and the diaspora were returning to celebrate a remarkable life lived by a loving, formidable and great lady.

I still meet up annually with Marvin, a good friend from Bluebell Common; sometimes he brings others whose stories aren't recorded here, but whose journeys could fill a book of their own. He'd rung me to tell me of Gloria's death and pass on the details of her funeral. I'd cancelled my client for that day and arranged to pick Marvin up, but he was ill that morning. I'd have no one to accompany me and I started to feel out of my comfort zone. How would I react, returning to the world that I'd left behind, like a butterfly shedding its cocoon? This would be a test of all the work I'd done to make

EPILOGUE

me whole again. To revisit the church where I'd preached and conducted worship so many times would indeed open a door that had been closed for some time. What would emerge from that place that had been closed off to me for so long?

I'd visited Gloria over the years, drifting in and out of her life, keeping in touch sharing family news, but those visits had dwindled as the pace of family life picked up.

I'd last seen her a year before and she'd clearly been deteriorating. Whilst I was there, a church warden came to share Holy Communion with her and I left, slightly disturbed at this up-close and personal experience of the world of faith. I didn't know how ill she'd become and it was now too late to give her one last hug and tell her "I love you."

I'd tried to reason why I felt so uneasy about returning to my first parish, but I couldn't reach any conclusions. It was troubling me that I might have unresolved issues and possibly still have work to do if I was to come to terms with my past and the decision I'd made to discard my faith like yesterday's newspaper. I knew that I'd come a long way, and yet the church still represented a failure to me. The culmination of years of bad choices, of drifting, of ignoring issues, of papering over the cracks, had seen me attempt to take my own life, and here I was walking back into the world that put me there.

It took some resolve to open the car door. I was tempted to drive on, go home, to pretend I'd been there, but no, that was not what I'd become. A growing sense of trepidation began to build, to make me question why I was there. My inner critic, silent for so long, had found its voice: "You see all these people? They know all about you, about what you became and how you walked away." But I'd come too far to give time or inner space to negativity. I was proud of what I'd achieved and confident in the new life I'd built.

As I approached the church steps, the place where I'd persuaded a drunken Dave to give up his attempts to enter the church, I realised the the man next to me was familiar. Three decades hadn't erased his smile. John was a former miner, and in worked in his spare time for the youth service, providing recreation, guidance and life-coaching for generations of young people failed by the system.

"Hey up, youth, how's tricks?" was his greeting. The ice was broken and my heart rate started to come down.

He found us two spaces at the back of a packed church. Now this was significant. In ministry, you tend to find that the older the deceased is, the fewer the mourners at their funeral. As extended families break up, work colleagues lose touch after retirement and peers begin to pass away themselves, the potential pool of attendees dwindles. But here, on this day, something remarkable was happening. A woman in her 90s had made such an impact on the lives of so many that there was standing room only in the large church: a measure of her remarkable service to those around her and a fitting tribute to her life.

Feeling a tap on my shoulder, I turned round to see an

EPILOGUE

unfamiliar face, but a familiar dog collar, my once coveted goal, around his neck. It was the current vicar.

"It's Seth, isn't it?" he enquired amicably.

"Yes, that's me," I replied.

"You've been pointed out to me and I wanted to say hello and thank you," he said.

"Thank me?" I asked.

"Yes, thank you for all you did for this parish and Bluebell Common. People still talk about those days and all you did. You certainly made your mark."

And with that he left me and went to robe up and start the service. Any doubts, any negativity, were dispelled as I realised that my actions, my ministry all those years ago, *had* made a difference, a lasting difference, and these people hadn't judged me for my fall, but had remembered me for what I'd done with and for them.

Another tap. This time it was a church warden telling me there was going to be an opportunity to say a few words about Gloria during the service, if I'd like to.

Would I? Really though, would I? I didn't know what to do. It could unlock all kinds of unresolved issues, speaking in church again, addressing a congregation. Perhaps the question I was posing myself was wrong, perhaps I needed to ask "Should I?" Was it a risk? Probably, but so far these people had been accepting and probably had been all along.

As the service began, we turned our thoughts to Gloria, remembering and celebrating all that she was to all those gathered in the church and beyond. It was a moving and fitting commemoration. She was getting a good send-off.

Towards the end of the service, the vicar announced the opportunity to say a few words in memory of Gloria and, without thinking about it, I found myself at the front of the church, where I'd led worship all those years ago.

The words flowed and I preached a very brief eulogy, which likened Gloria to the embodiment of unconditional, strong, warm and unselfish love.

As I sat down, I realised I may have pushed another door open and didn't know what would be on the other side.

The service ended with a standing ovation and cheers for Gloria and all that she was. An unusual conclusion for an extraordinary woman.

We all stood up as her coffin was carried by her sons out to the hearse, with her family following on for a private burial. As the congregation began to disperse, several parishioners approached me to say hello and satisfy their curiosity about what I was doing and how I was. But one person hung back and waited until I was alone. A lady I recognised, but couldn't put a name to, came up to me and smiled. "I've never forgot what you did for me," she said.

Unfortunately, I had. "Just doing my job," I replied, desperately trying to recall what it was I'd done; it was clearly significant to her, but it was lost in three decades of fog.

EPILOGUE

"It was after Bible study," she related. "I was two days into a migraine and had dragged myself along; I never miss it, you know. You noticed I wasn't right and you asked me about it, you always seemed to notice. When I told you, you said that we couldn't have that, could we?"

A glimmer of recognition sparked a memory, but it was still too vague for me to give it any meaning.

"You took me into the Lady Chapel and prayed for me," she said, now beaming. "And I want you to know that I haven't had a migraine since."

I can't overstate the positive influence Gloria's funeral and the words people said had on me. I'd been welcomed back into the family of the church.

From my re-birth and up to this special day, I could rationalise away that urge we have as humans to make meaning of ourselves and our place in the universe by referring to God. To me, the search for a sense of belonging and meaning was over. I believed that if anyone is looking for that sense of the divine, if their inner self is yearning for fulfilment from another source, then they can find that in the beauty of the landscape around them. In the murmuring of a moorland stream I hear a voice that has spoken for millions of years and will continue long after I'm gone. In the eyes and in the touch of our children we can experience and know the eternal; we're not consigned to oblivion, but part of us lives on in our children and their children too. But, on that day, something began to change in me.

The welcome I'd received from the family of the church and the certainty of that lady's story of the banishing of debilitating migraines has made me think again.

Did that healing really take place?

Had God begun to work to overturn my skepticism?

I don't know. But I've pushed the door open and stepped inside – and I've started to smile again.

Acknowledgements

I would like to acknowledge the help of my wife and family in writing this book. They have given me the time, space and permission to go away and work on it.

I specifically would like to thank Jo for her faith in this project and inciteful input, it is greatly appreciated.

Neil, you will never know the depth of my gratitude for offering me an opportunity that enabled me to afford to spend the time on this project.

Al, you have been a friend from the beginning of this project and I thank you for the friendship that has stood the test of time.

Bill, you were there to help pick me up when I fell, you are indeed a brother.

I would like to acknowledge the gifts that my Mother and Father have given to me over the years. The love from my Mum and the joy of the outdoors shared by my Dad are constant companions.

FAITHLESS

Finally, I would like to thank you, dear reader, for opening these pages and sharing some of my experiences with me.

Peace and Light
Seth